The Great Opportunity

What Leaders Throughout the Vocations Are Saying About *The Great Opportunity*

"If you are new to the term 'vocational disciple making' you have found the right guide in Dave Buehring. *The Great Opportunity* both gives vision for how this concept can change the world and reveals how it is key to engaging a new generation with the truth of God's calling for each of our lives. An essential read for any person of faith."

Gabe Lyons
President of Q Ideas & Author of *Good Faith*

"Dave Buehring is a seasoned spiritual leader that has the experience and authority to give you a powerful gift in this easy-to-read book that will inform, inspire, and ignite you to action into one of the greatest missing keys for the transformation of the nation and the world for Jesus and His Kingdom. Jesus said, 'Go, disciple all nations.' Dave writes how in *The Great Opportunity!*"

Loren Cunningham
Founder, Youth With a Mission (YWAM)

"Dave Buehring has been my friend for a long time. It is wonderful to see his dedication to being a disciple of Jesus and his focus on the mission of making disciples of Jesus in every vocation throughout society. His mission is also meant to be our mission. In *The Great Opportunity*, Dave shares with us why and then shows us how."

Scott Hamilton
Olympic Figure Skating Gold Medalist and Commentator
Scott Hamilton CARES Foundation

"Dave's heart for disciple making is inspiring and desperately needed today, both in the church and throughout the vocations. I've benefited greatly from people pouring into my life. I have seen its value in my walk with the Lord and I have a heart to do the same for others. I highly recommend *The Great Opportunity* and definitely encourage disciple making!"

Jeremy Camp
Musician & Author, Founder of Speaking Louder Ministries

"For the last 15 years, Dave Buehring has discipled me to reflect the ways of God in my platform of the music industry. I am now making disciples through my 'Sisters' group of female Christian artists. In *The Great Opportunity*, Dave lovingly and practically equips you how to walk out the Great Commission in the same way that he taught me."

Mandisa
American Idol Finalist
GRAMMY Winning Artist

"A great book on making disciples should not merely be the product of a mind. It should also be the product of a life, one devoted to fashioning souls in the image of Jesus. Dave Buehring has lived this kind of life, and so he has been able to give us this kind of book. May we use *The Great Opportunity* to change our generation."

Stephen Mansfield, Ph.D.
New York Times Bestselling Author
Founder of GreatMan

"*The Great Opportunity* addresses a glaring need that can still plague the Body of Christ: the sacred-secular divide. Dave Buehring shows us how to join God in the work of seeing people's lives transformed into the image of Jesus in the context of our everyday lives at work. I highly recommend this book to anyone who desires their work week to be right on the cutting edge of the Gospel!"

Eddie Broussard
International Vice President, The Navigators

"I grew up in a Christian church where being a pastor was the only job that was valued. That's a common error in American Christianity, and it's produced a multitude of injurious downstream effects, inside the faith and in the country. Dave Buehring's passion is to help every person discover the ways that their unique talents and personalities are part of a bigger story and have divine purpose. *The Great Opportunity* is aimed at helping Christians be agents of service — especially to those who are most in need and on the margins — rather than seeking conquest and domination."

Jon Ward
Political Reporter, Yahoo News

"I'm so glad that Dave Buehring finally wrote down what he's been teaching me for many years. The biblical principles on vocational disciple making in Dave's book, *The Great Opportunity,* have changed the way I think and how I live out the purpose of disciple making in the NFL locker room."

Kent Chevalier
Chaplain, Pittsburgh Steelers

In *The Great Opportunity*, Dave Buehring inspires us to view our vocation as a God-given calling and envisions us to see a world that is shaped and molded by the ways of God. Buehring challenges us to see our marketplace as our mission and our job as a ministry. He gives us practical tools to personally walk in the ways of Jesus and to shape others in the ways of Jesus. This is a must-read for every follower of Jesus and every leader who wishes to disciple others in the ways of Jesus."

Heather Zempel
Discipleship Pastor, National Community Church
Washington, D.C.

"After fighting for my country, my entry into politics and government was also out of a desire to serve. It's a calling rooted in my faith and how God made me. I've been blessed to have a Christian who has worked in this world walk alongside me and guide me as I try to make decisions based on Biblical principles. *The Great Opportunity* will help me do the same for others who work in my field."

Senator Joshua Revak
State Senate, Alaska
Former Main Battle Tank Crew Member, U.S. Army

"Dave Buehring was born to write this book. In *The Great Opportunity*, he makes the case that the Great Commission isn't just about making disciples of Jesus in our churches, but also in the vocations where God has placed us. Dave delivers both a convincing vision and a compelling plan – something that every pastor should want their flock to understand and undertake!"

Steve Berger
Senior Pastor, Grace Chapel
Franklin, Tennessee

"Dave Buehring beautifully lays out for readers the biblical call for reproducing ourselves. *The Great Opportunity* will challenge and excite you about making disciples in your family and may result in a paradigm shift regarding others with whom you journey through life. A must-read for every Jesus follower, no matter what your vocation in society may be."

Paris Goodyear-Brown, LCSW, RPT-S
Child and Family Therapist, Author and Speaker

"*The Great Opportunity* provides a description of what it means to raise-up disciple makers in the various spheres of life. It is very practical and real-world, revealing decades of experience by one of the country's top disciple making leaders."

Bobby Harrington, D.Min
Point Leader of Discipleship.org and Renew.org

"*The Great Opportunity* is a breakthrough book addressing the Great Co-mission of Jesus in the world of work. From teaching the importance of calling to the power of relationship to the need for obedience, it teaches us how to be the disciple makers Jesus calls us to be. Dave Buehring has written a treasure of a book that is packed with practical wisdom, experience, and encouragement."

Phyllis Hendry Halverson
Inaugural President/CEO of Lead Like Jesus

"Long before it was popular, Dave Buehring was encouraging us to make disciples. In *The Great Opportunity* you will find well-researched, intelligent and practical steps we can all implement, regardless of our vocation!"

John McB. Hodgson, MD, MSCAI, FACC
Director of Cardiology, Wilson Health
Professor of Medicine, Case Western Reserve
School of Medicine

"Many see work as something that takes us away from our faith rather than as a calling where we can represent and glorify God. Women in the workplace desire to bring their whole selves wherever they spend each hour of their days, including their workplaces. *The Great Opportunity* both inspires and equips Christians to make God known while serving Him in the professional world."

Diane Paddison
Founder and Executive Director of 4word
Author of *Work, Love, Pray*
Former Global Executive,
Fortune 500 and Fortune 1000 Companies

"As a Christian living and working in Silicon Valley, it is challenging to spread the message of Jesus. But believers can and should pursue careers in science and technology because our work matters to God. Biblical ethics and morality are needed when dealing with issues of privacy and the proper use of artificial intelligence. *The Great Opportunity* provides an essential blueprint for starting the discussion on how our vocational calling can honor God."

Jim Chiang
Senior Director, Artificial Intelligence
Engineer and Data Scientist

"The first job God ever gave us is to steward His creation. That responsibility hasn't gone away. Christians should be at the forefront of advancing science, technology and energy innovation all for the benefit of the environment. In doing so, we can help solve the world's greatest earthly challenges while pointing people to the Only One who can solve our deepest spiritual challenges. *The Great Opportunity* provides valuable insights and practical ideas about how we can live out those mutual callings.

Drew Bond
CEO, PowerField Energy Inc.
Co-Founder & CEO, C3 Solutions

"With a friend like Dave Buehring, there is nothing you enjoy more than those too few times when you get to be together, and have a deep, life-giving chat about things that really matter. Reading The Great Opportunity provides you with that kind of experience as Dave converses with you deeply about your core calling: being a whole-hearted and whole-minded disciple of Jesus in the context of life where He has placed you."

Rev. David R. Wells M.A., D.D.
General Superintendent
The Pentecostal Assemblies of Canada

THE
GREAT
OPPORTUNITY

Making Disciples of Jesus
in *Every* Vocation

DAVE BUEHRING

NASHVILLE

NEW YORK • LONDON • MELBOURNE • VANCOUVER

THE GREAT OPPORTUNITY
Making Disciples of Jesus in *Every* Vocation

Published in New York, New York, by Morgan James Publishing. Morgan James is a trademark of Morgan James, LLC. www.MorganJamesPublishing.com

Unless otherwise indicated, all Scripture quotations are from the ESV® Bible (The Holy Bible, English Standard Version®), copyright © 2001 by Crossway, a publishing ministry of Good News Publishers. Used by permission. All rights reserved.

When indicated, some Scripture quotations taken from The Holy Bible, New International Version® NIV®, Copyright © 1973 1978 1984 2011 by Biblica, Inc. TM Used by permission. All rights reserved worldwide.

ISBN 9781631951794 paperback
ISBN 9781631951800 eBook
Library of Congress Control Number: 2020938146

Cover and Interior Design by:
Chris Treccani
www.3dogcreative.net

Morgan James is a proud partner of Habitat for Humanity Peninsula and Greater Williamsburg. Partners in building since 2006.

Get involved today! Visit
MorganJamesPublishing.com/giving-back

TABLE OF CONTENTS

ACKNOWLEDGMENTS

I want to begin by thanking my Mom and Dad for pointing me to Jesus, aiming me towards my life mission, and regularly praying for me throughout my life's journey.

I am grateful to both Loren Cunningham and Winkie Pratney, faith fathers in my life since I was eighteen. Loren, I am grateful for God using you to place within my heart Jesus' mandate of disciple making, and the vision for impacting the spheres of society. Winkie, thank you for your encouragement and counsel over the years, and our many conversations around what you have referred to, and entitled your book on the subject, as the "spiritual vocations".

Thank you to our Lionshare Team, both staff and board, for your ongoing encouragement and help in launching this book. Special thanks to Darren and Sonya Bearson, my companions in the vision and work of Lionshare. Your counsel and hard work have contributed much to this book and all that we do together to impact generations, vocations, and nations!

My gratitude also goes to hundreds of my friends—way too many to name here, but you know who you are—who have labored with me for many years over disciple making and the vocations. You helped refine my thinking and articulate this so much better. Thank you.

I am very thankful for my relationship with Morgan James Publishing and its fine team, led by David L. Hancock. Thanks so much to Jim Howard and Karen Anderson. I appreciate your heart and your hard work on behalf of me, this book, and Lionshare. I'm also grateful for your vision of where this could go to serve and impact many.

Sissi Haner, I appreciate your gracious and skilled hand in the editing process. Thank you for the way you have made my rough places smooth and framed my words so they can mean the most. Your help to me is greatly valued and much appreciated.

Dwight Marable, thank you for lending me your beautiful cabin to write. It was the perfect getaway, allowing me to listen to the Lord and get what was in my heart on paper.

Troy Birdsong, thanks for the graphics you created to help people "see" things better.

I especially want to thank the love of my life, my wife, Cheryl. You have walked by my side for four decades now, experiencing the insights involved, the mistakes made, the lessons learned, and the ways of God that have been put into practice that make up this book. Thank you for your love, immeasurable help, and prayers. This book would not be possible without you.

Finally, to our four grandchildren, Baron, Baylor, Nolan, and Alana, the sons and daughters of our incredible kids, Ryan and Kyndall Buehring, and Malia and Eric Holman. As one of the greatest delights of my life, you are part of the reason why I have written this book. I often think of you, knowing that although my eyes may never see what I've written here fully come to pass, yours just may! My Papa heart regular prays for you, and my hope is that one day when you grow up, that you too will read this, and discover God's amazing path for your life to change the world! I love you very much.

FOREWORD

Many books about discipleship and disciple making read like car manuals, in which the description of all the right parts does *not* make for the joy of motoring. Not this book! Disciple making has been treated by many as if it was the responsibility of those in ministry or, at best, as an extracurricular activity. This book recovers it as the vocational calling for all disciples: no ifs, ands or buts. Dave Buehring presents an applicable, assessable, and achievable vision and practice for what he describes as "four-generation-deep" disciple making. Welcome to the rest of your effective life for God!

Many of us, including the author, were influenced by the groundbreaking book by Os Guinness, *The Call*, in which he wrote: "Calling is not only a matter of being and doing what we are but also of becoming what we are not yet but are called by God to be." This book carries the same DNA. It is rooted in the character of God and in our relationship with Him. It is grounded in scriptural study and meditation, founded on a biblical theology of work and calling, and earthed in the proven reality of the author's own discipleship. Dave Buehring possesses the attested experience and humble authority as a disciple maker of thousands!

There is no reader who is so spiritually mature or so ministry-experienced who will not be biblically instructed and equipped by this treatise. Volumes of wisdom and revelation are compressed into these pages, a power-packed concentrate of truth, drawing you into an encouraging, reasonable, inviting, inspiring, motivating, compelling exhortation and a very pastoral and thoughtful conversation.

The fact is that we are being "disciple-made" as we read! There are many books that we put down when finished, with good intentions to do something about what we just engaged. Again, not this one!

You will conclude your reading feeling confirmed as a disciple and affirmed as a disciple maker. You will be re-commissioned to fulfill your calling, mature in character, develop competencies and pledge your commitment to be a disciple of Jesus who invites all in the gravitational pull of your life to become "disciple-made," too. As you walk away from this book, you will be walking already prepared and primed into an expectant and renewed vocational calling as a disciple maker. Thank you, Lord; thank you, Dave; and thank you to the publishers who had the discernment and the vision to get this book into our hands and hearts at this moment of "prophetic timeliness."

*~ **Stuart McAlpine***
Senior Pastor, Christ Our Shepherd Church, Washington, D.C.
International Director, ASK NETWORK
Senior Teaching Fellow, The C.S. Lewis Institute

INTRODUCTION

And Jesus came and said to them, "All authority in heaven and on earth has been given to me. Go therefore and make disciples of all nations, baptizing them in the name of the Father and of the Son and of the Holy Spirit, teaching them to observe all that I have commanded you. And behold, I am with you always, to the end of the age." (Matthew 28:18–20)

If we could rewind time and be present in that very moment when these words of the Great Co-Mission fell from Jesus' mouth into the ears of His disciples, I think we would better understand how they heard it. In the context of their journey with Jesus, it would have likely translated to them as: *What I've lived and poured into you the last three years—just go and do that with others!*

When looking at The Book of Acts—which we will a little later—we see these same disciples carrying on this disciple making mission of Jesus. As a matter of fact, disciple making was their primary mission, it's how they launched the Church, and it radically changed their world!

Have you ever considered that our families, communities, country, and the world are in the condition they are in because we, as followers of Jesus, have disobeyed His last command to make disciples? I like how my long-time friend Randy Young says it, "It's like Jesus' last command has become our least concern!" That "least concern" has had lots of consequences, both in our world and in His Church.

Our daily headlines reveal a world that has totally lost its moorings! Constant culture clashes over values. Extreme reactions in reply to initial overreactions. Authority figures routinely destroying trust with those they are supposed to be leading and serving. Unresolved racial injustice and inequity. A global pandemic presenting challenges on both personal and national levels. Massive confusion over things forever held as true. And, today's leadership equation often has nothing to do with character, competency, and connecting well with others, but instead looks more like this: Little experience + lots of loud opinions + leveraged social media = A leader people should follow!

What about the Church, Jesus' deeply loved and blood-shed-for Bride?

We are likely living amongst one of the most scripturally illiterate generations in all of history. This has created a "spiritual thinness" and powerlessness among God's precious flock. At times, the lives behind the voices leading today's Church are often unproven, lacking tested character and the seasoned wisdom of the ways of God. We have disciples disavowing their faith yet are being applauded and promoted based on their unfaithfulness to Jesus and the Scriptures. We've lost our way in being both true to Jesus while also winning the world to Him. Then there's the rootless, creative, multi-gifted, and wonderful next generation, who are very drawn to Jesus but are not so sure of His Church.

Jesus, revealed and reflected through His Church, is still the answer to the world's greatest issues, needs, and challenges! The Church is still His Beloved Bride, the love of His life that He sacrificed everything for. However, she won't be able to fully function like He dreamed about unless we recalibrate to His Great Co-Mission of making disciples makers.

Think about it with me. Jesus asked His disciples to reproduce His character, ways, and mission in others who would follow Him. This allows disciples to carry the heart, attitudes, words, and actions of Jesus into every setting and situation of life they find themselves in. This includes their families, relationships—and within their vocations!

Herein lies the great opportunity!

Without connecting our calling and the Great Co-Mission, our vocation and disciple making, how can we ever disciple people to reveal and reflect the life of Jesus so that His Kingdom is advanced and those around us practically experience His grace and goodness?

- How can a business owner, who sincerely loves Jesus, understand that their "bottom line" is much more than just dollars and cents without someone discipling them to think and act out of scriptural values?
- Without developing disciples in the media who view life through the lens of the ways of God, how can we really expect truth and inspirational stories to replace biased reporting and constant divisive analysis?
- Unless we pour God's ways into our artists and athletes, instead of using their God-given gifts and platform to glorify His name and serve as examples to young people, we can expect even more self-focused adulation and the exaltation of selfish living.

- How will we ever have a president or prime minister of a nation governing in the ways of God if no one has discipled them to reflect God's character in their attitudes, words, and actions, and to reference His ways in their decision making?

- Unless pastors and churches are discipled around the character, ways, and mission of Jesus, the impact of faulty foundations and the ongoing trend of spiritual thinness will impact generations well beyond our lifetimes.

The changes we desire to see in our lives, families, churches, vocations, and societies don't just happen automatically. They happen because of the deliberate reproducing of disciples.

Vocational disciple making. This is likely a new and, possibly, an odd word combination to you. If you're like most people that I know, these two ideas—vocation and disciple making—have never met in your heart or mind before.

It is interesting to note that three out of four Christian workers do not connect faith with their work.[1] According to David Kinnaman, president of Barna Group, "A failure to provide vocational discipleship could be a failure to help Christians, especially younger ones, keep their faith."[2] Speaking of discipling Millennials, Barna Group's research revealed that 65% believe that God gave them certain gifts and talents to use for His glory; 67% of them want to use their gifts and talents for the good of others; and 37% wish they had a clearer understanding of how they should use their gifts and talents to serve God.[3] Talk about a great opportunity to shape a generation regarding connecting their calling with the Great Co-Mission of disciple making!

As we begin our journey through this book together, we'll take a fresh look at calling and vocation. Then, in the second half of the book, we'll look at the disciple making blueprint of Jesus, how He did it, and how you can engage it too! Also, to help you get your arms around making disciples in your vocation, I begin each chapter with a story from my life or about friends (whose names I have changed) that I've had a hand in discipling and who have practically applied God's ways within their vocations. Later, you'll find an entire chapter dedicated to more stories to help you see the kind of fruit that can result from blending your calling with the Great Co-Mission, your vocation, and disciple making.

This book is aimed at envisioning, equipping, and engaging you in one of the greatest opportunities that you'll have in your lifetime. I trust that the Holy Spirit will reveal much to you, helping you to personally connect your calling with the Great Co-Mission, your vocation with reproducing disciple makers. This is how we can participate with Jesus in bringing real and meaningful change to the people we love and the world we live in.

Be very careful, then, how you live—not as unwise but as wise, making the most of every opportunity, because the days are evil. Therefore do not be foolish, but understand what the Lord's will is. (Ephesians 5:15–17 NIV)

~ *Dave Buehring*

CHAPTER 1

A Divine Design

When I was twenty years old, I worked with Youth With A Mission (YWAM) on the Big Island of Hawai'i. I had been living there for two years, and my role revolved around relating to and reaching teenagers, from about a dozen ethnic backgrounds, living around the island. Alongside my team, we traveled up to 600 miles each week to be on eight high school campuses. Our ministry, called Acts 2, ran a Christian club on campus over the lunch hour, hosted three to four annual island-wide retreats, led summer international youth discipleship camps, participated in Kona's community youth council, and extended our reach to youth on the other Hawaiian Islands, as well as to Brazil and Australia.

It was an exciting time in my life, a time of growing and stretching. While faithfully serving Hawai'i's youth, I was also considering my gifts and calling, and what that would mean in the long run. Many questions percolated to the top of my heart and mind, like:

What are my gifts?

What does fruitfulness look like?

What vocational field is God calling me to?

What shaping will I need to reflect Jesus and fulfill my calling?

How does what I am called to do connect with Jesus' Great Co-Mission?

In the midst of this season of time, I was invited to visit with Peter Jordan, a Canadian whom I had built a friendship with during my time in Kona. Peter was an older, wiser follower of Jesus, and he was also the personal assistant to Loren Cunningham, YWAM's founder and president. As we visited that day, he shared that Loren needed someone to travel with him throughout the country to talk with people, after he had finished speaking, who wanted to know more about YWAM. He asked if I would be open and interested in doing that!

Needless to say, I was honored to be asked. And, trust me, it didn't take me long to hear from heaven regarding this opportunity! Not only would I be able to have the privilege of serving him, but I was also looking forward to gleaning all that I could from this seasoned man of God!

About a month later, I joined Loren on a trip that would take us to Dallas, Los Angeles, and Washington, D.C. Sure enough, just like we had talked about, Loren would teach, and I would hand out information and answer people's questions about how to get more involved in our mission.

One day, while visiting on one of our flights, Loren asked me what I thought my gifts were. To be honest, at twenty years of age, I was still in the process of figuring that out myself! I hemmed and hawed a bit and then took my best shot at it. He said that after watching me over the last couple of years, he saw both a leadership quality and a teaching gift in me, which was very self-affirming. Little did I know that what he was about to say next would mark my life from that moment up to now!

You know, Dave, it really isn't important how big the organizations are that you will lead or the size of the groups that you will teach. The way that God will measure the fruitfulness of your life is how you invested to the third and fourth generations.

Wow, talk about needing a minute to take that all in!

Up some 40,000 feet in the air, in just a couple of sentences, gifts, calling and the Great Co-Mission, and generational fruitfulness are all dropped on me!

Loren then referenced Paul's words to a young leader in 2 Timothy 2:2, reflecting four generations' deep disciple making (Paul—Timothy—Faithful Ones—Others). He was challenging me about how I was going to use my God-given gifts and calling to produce fruitfulness in and through my life. It was a whole new grid for me to look at life through!

My gifts tied to generational fruitfulness.
My calling connected to the Great Co-Mission.
Reproducing disciple makers through my vocation.

Since that trip, now forty years ago, I clearly see God's divine design as I've connected my calling and the Great Co-Mission!

As I've applied disciple making within my vocation in the various seasons of my life, I've had the joy and privilege of meeting those third and fourth generation disciples Loren talked with me about on that flight, and in a few cases, even my fifth and sixth!

*****

The world awaits.

As followers of Jesus, we may be living in one of the greatest times in history to impact the lives of people, serve the needs of families and communities, and transform entire societies. Never has there been the combination of resources, technology, mobility, creativity, societal ripeness, and the experience and skill of people to accomplish so much for so many!

But to make that kind of mark on the world around us, we must recalibrate to some cores that will allow us to see clearly, function fully, and work well together.

The current culture of extreme busyness, packed schedules, and no margin leans us toward being so exhausted that rising early in the morning to seek the face of God seems unreasonable. Trying to make ends meet, tending our families and often running on empty because of demands at work hinders us from even considering how our vocation blends with God's purposes. And, the climate of contentiousness, easy offenses, and "solo flying" causes us to miss opportunities of teaming together to benefit the lives in real need around us—and around the world!

With that being said—you and me—we've been born for such a time as this!

When God gets hold of a man or a woman whose heart has become fully His, there is no limit to what He can do in and through their life. This theme is repeated over and over in the

Scriptures—from Abraham to Joshua to Deborah to Daniel to Esther—and in the New Testament with people like Mary, Peter, Barnabas, Paul, and Priscilla. Within every generation, God sets his hand on available and obedient hearts to rouse His Church, upend the culture, shake the nations, and accomplish His Kingdom purposes!

And yet, the world is waiting.

Waiting for what?

Waiting to see if it's REALLY TRUE that God loves the world so much that He sends His Son through His people to provide for the poor, comfort the hurting, help the hopeless, free the enslaved, rescue the refugees, serve justice, heal marriages, restore relationships, revive communities, ignite economies, govern righteously, fulfill purposes, and restore joy where it has been snatched away!

The world is waiting for and desperately needs the People of God to function like His Church in the way that Jesus dreamed she can!

Yet, in our hearts and minds, that seems nearly impossible, too idealistic, so impractical. It can get quite overwhelming just thinking about where to even begin to head down that road! It feels like the challenge of a million lifetimes… like something…

…only God could conceive a plan for!

A divine design that is…

So masterful, that it can touch every person and impact every nation!

So all-encompassing, that it includes and involves every single one of us!

So wise, that it pulls out of us what God has already placed within us!

So simple, that it can be missed because of overly busy and complicated lives!

So incomprehensible, that it can only be done by depending on God's Presence!

So weighted with fruitfulness, that it can transform lives and change the world!

This divine design was implemented by Jesus as He walked this planet. It transformed the lives of a dozen guys who, with other transformed men and women, changed their world!

It has been said about these disciples of Jesus:

> *These men who have turned the world upside down*
> *have come here also...* Acts 17:6

What is this divine design?
What does it have to do with me?
How can I participate in it?

Your Calling

Have you ever paused to consider your calling, where Jesus has uniquely appointed you to serve on behalf of Himself and His Kingdom within society? Another way to ask this is, how does Jesus express Himself through you as His personal ambassador to the world around you?

According to the Barna Group, six out of ten working Christian adults believe they've been given certain skills and talents to use for God's glory or for the good of others, and one in three wants to know more about how they could serve God through their talents.[1] In their research, they also found the word "calling" is first associated with ministering to or serving others, with a subtle perceived hierarchy with ministry-related vocations at the top, and others at the bottom. Here is what they found among those surveyed where they believe there is "usually a calling"[2]:

- Pastor–69%
- Missionary–67%
- Worship Leader–59%
- Parent–52%
- Church Staff (other than pastor–44%
- Firefighter–37%
- Pediatrician–36%
- Musician–32%
- Military Officer–30%
- Athlete–25%
- Plastic Surgeon–20%
- Financial Advisor–11%
- Accountant–11%
- School Janitor–6%

This is amazing to me! I have walked with folks who serve in the bottom two-thirds of this list and am I ever grateful that they see God's hands on them in and through their vocations! Imagine the impact of a godly school janitor, knowing he was likely the only person in the whole school who got to pray every day on the job over every seat of every student for God to bless their lives! Or, the financial advisor whose experience reshapes someone's future. What about the plastic surgeon who uses his skills to make it easier for a burn victim to live life and face others? God's grace, wisdom, and compassion at work in and through vocations!

I have a good friend, now in heaven, who served for many years as an Army General. He knew God's call on his life in this role, serving several of our nation's presidents. He told me how dependent he was on the Lord as he trained and deployed his troops, and how prayer at his desk was a daily part of his life! His call by God to protect the people of our nation—influencing and affecting millions more people than my life will likely ever touch—is just as significant as those called to represent Jesus in the nations as missionaries! This is no different than God's call upon Joshua, Deborah, and David in Scripture who were anointed to battle on Israel's behalf!

You see, you were not made by the hands of our Creator to simply spend 40–60 hours each week "going to work," "having a job so I can get paid," or even work within "a career that I like." Rather, according to Psalm 139:14–15, you were "wonderfully made" and "intricately wrought." From the original Old Testament language of Hebrew, that means "distinguished wonderfully" and "diversely embroidered." You have been created amazingly extraordinary, distinctive, and have woven within you all the necessary and colorful ingredients you need to fulfill what you have been born to be and do!

Yet, it is interesting to me that the average worker will spend some 90,000 hours "on the clock" throughout their lifetimes[3], and among working adults, 75% are looking for a way to live a more meaningful life![4] From God's perspective, our vocations and the many hours given there are to be a beautiful blend of using our talents in a way that fulfill God's purposes and benefit the lives of others. As a result, this can also bring great meaning to our own lives!

I find that we often use words like work, job, profession, career, occupation, and vocation, thinking they all mean the same thing. However, the word "calling" is rooted in the Latin word *vocatio*, from which we get in English, the word "vocation." Jesus has intended that our vocation be a primary way of expressing our calling!

Tucked inside of you, by your Divine Designer, are natural abilities, acquired skills, and spiritual gifts meant to better advance Jesus' Kingdom, bless the lives of people, and bring Him great glory! None of us are meant to "sit on the sidelines" or to sit on the curb and "watch the parade go by"! Every single person who has or will ever be conceived carries the breath of their Maker, and their lives are intended to make a difference in our world.

The lives of people and nations throughout history have been greatly marked by the vocational callings of followers of Jesus! Here are just a few examples:

- Michael Faraday (1791–1867) was an English scientist who discovered electromagnetic induction, the principle behind the electric transformer and generator. It is largely due to his efforts that electricity became practical for use in the technology that we use today!

- Author Harriet Beecher Stowe (1811–1896) wrote *Uncle Tom's Cabin*, highlighting the plight of slaves in America. Upon meeting her for the first time, President Abraham Lincoln said, "So you're the little woman who wrote the book that started this great (civil) war."

- Susanna Wesley (1669–1742), whose vocation was motherhood, had nineteen children, two of whom became noted evangelists: John, who was known for his sermons, and Charles, who became known for his hymns. The Wesleyans and Methodists are their spiritual offspring.

- Displaying tremendous courage and poise, Jackie Robinson (1919–1972) broke the baseball color line by playing for the Brooklyn Dodgers. His #42 jersey was retired across all Major League Baseball teams, becoming the first pro athlete in any sport to be so honored.

- Corrie ten Boom (1892–1983), a Dutch watchmaker who, with her family, helped Jews escape the Nazi Holocaust during World War II by hiding them in her home. For this, she served time in a German concentration camp.
- Born into a wealthy family, William Wilberforce (1759–1833), who could have easily passed on getting involved, instead, as a British politician, significantly contributed to the end of the international slave trade.

A scientist, an author, a mom, an athlete, a businesswoman, and a government leader. Each one, as followers of Jesus, contributed distinctively to making a difference in the life of an individual, a family, or a society.

The Great Co-Mission

When Jesus was here, He demonstrated how to walk with His Father, love people well, and live a life of obedience that allowed the Kingdom of God to be advanced. His daily desire was to be so in tune with His Father that, whatever His Father wanted, He'd be available to do.

Nothing was as important to Jesus as His relationship with His Father. Early mornings, late nights, in the middle of the day, His disciples would find Him seeking the face of His Father, enjoying His companionship, listening for His voice, and following His lead.

As an overflow of relationship with His Father, Jesus' vision was both clear and captivating: reconciling relationships and redeeming people's lives—then inviting the reconciled and redeemed to team with Him to do the same for others!

Jesus has firsthand experience implementing the divine design, molding and mobilizing the lives of the reconciled and redeemed to change the world. A fresh read-through of the Book of Acts will erase any questions of what He is capable of with hearts that are fully His!

As a missionary with Youth With A Mission (YWAM), in my late teens to mid-twenties, I began to more closely encounter "The Great Commission" found in Matthew 28:18–20:

And Jesus came and said to them, "All authority in heaven and on earth has been given to me. Go therefore and make disciples of all nations, baptizing them in the name of the Father and of the Son and of the Holy Spirit, teaching them to observe all that I have commanded you. And behold, I am with you always, to the end of the age."

Go.

Make disciples.

Of all nations.

Baptizing them in the Name of the Father, Son and Holy Spirit.

Teaching them to obey all that I have commanded you.

I am with you always.

Considering where we began, just a little bit ago, I think we already have a pretty good handle on the "great" part of "The Great Commission," as the world's needs and the task at hand can certainly be defined as that!

But what about the second part of this familiar phrase, "commission"?

Over the years, I began to view this "invitation command" of Jesus as an opportunity to "co-mission" with Him. To be on mission with Him. Together. His mission, now my mission. He leads, I follow. How He wants to get it done, is how I'm going to do it.

As we've noted, Jesus' mission was all about reconciling relationships and redeeming people's lives—then having them do the same for others. By reconciling relationships, I mean both people to God and people with one another. When I speak of redeeming people's lives, I mean God releasing them from their stuck places so they are free to walk in His ways and fully join in His purposes.

Think about the privilege of this for a moment: we—you and me—get to co-mission with Jesus in His divine design!

Now, there is one other very important part to this. One that is too often neglected. Once we're reconciled and redeemed, we are invited to also co-mission with Jesus to do the same for others!

The process that Jesus used of moving people from being reconciled and redeemed themselves to making them ready to come alongside others to experience the same is called disciple making.

Disciple making was and remains Jesus' original plan to change the world! While teaching the multitudes, healing the sick, and doing good wherever He went—His priority was making disciples of twelve men! It remains His primary way of advancing His Kingdom.

Jesus desires to turn the reconciled and redeemed into reproducible disciple makers! He wants to disciple them to reflect His character, walk in His ways, and participate in His mission so they can help others do the same for generations to come.

It's what Jesus did. And, it's what He's asked us to do too.

It's not The Great Suggestion.

It's The Great Co-Mission!

Connecting Your Calling and The Great Co-Mission

This book is about connecting your calling with Jesus' Great Co-Mission, something our Lionshare team refers to as *vocational disciple making*. Now, before I share with you what that means, I want you to first understand what it is not.

There is a wonderful growing quantity of excellent material on being "salt and light" on the job so that those who've not yet met Jesus may be introduced to Him, impacting their lives and eternity. This is incredibly important and desperately needed, but this is not what I mean by vocational disciple making.

Growing someone into spiritual maturity is vital for all who come to Jesus. This expression of disciple making is known as formational disciple making (more on this later). This is absolutely essential, and really, we simply can't function effectively as the Church without it! However, this too is not what I mean by vocational disciple making.

So, what is vocational disciple making?

Vocational disciple making is developing disciples of Jesus who reflect His character, walk in His ways, and participate in His mission, in and through their vocation.

Read that through another time or two.

Now, let me break this down a bit so we are on the same page.

First, vocational disciple making is about deliberately "developing" disciples of Jesus. Growth, maturity, and the ability to pass spiritual truths on to others does not happen accidentally. I've often teased that I wish we could just go to bed at night and, like dew found on morning grass, we could wake up with a light coating of "spiritual maturity dew" on us and call it good! However, it doesn't work that way, as it requires purposeful intentionality to develop someone as a disciple.

Second, part of defining vocational disciple making revolves around shaping the lives of disciples of Jesus so they more accurately "reflect Him" to the world around them. We are meant to reflect to others what He reveals about Himself. This is how people can "see" and "experience" what Jesus is really like! When "on the job," are our motivations, attitudes, words, and actions reflective of Jesus? How about the quality or excellence related to how we perform our work? The way we relate to those we work with? Do we reflect Jesus?

Now, we come to three specific areas of our deliberate discipling.

1. Reflecting His Character—Many people have a very difficult time seeing who Jesus is and what He is really like. You and I have the distinct privilege of showing them more personally what He is like as we reflect His kindness, faithfulness, integrity, grace, truth, hard work, justice, forgiveness, hope, compassion, etc., through our vocational role.

2. Walking in His Ways—His ways are "how He does things." Within our vocations, does how we relate, forgive, honor, and serve people reflect Jesus? What about how we make decisions, walk under authority, or fire people? How about walking in truths at work like honesty, justice, spiritual warfare, and the Fear of the Lord? Do you humbly (and quietly) apply the ways of Jesus in and through your job?

3. Participating in His Mission—Co-missioning with Jesus! His mission is always about people! So, considering the products and/or services that are tied to your vocation, and the unique gifts and abilities He has given you, how does

He express His care of those you work with through you? Do you "go to work" each day referencing how Jesus may want to better and bless the lives of others through your life?

There is one more piece to our vocational disciple making description, the phrase "in and through their vocation." Think about this as allowing Jesus to maximize the gifts and experiences He has placed within you, both when you are "at work" (in) as well as in a broader way (through) that can also advance His Kingdom.

For example, some friends of mine are incredibly handy. They love using their many tools to fix, repair, restore, add on to—whatever it takes to make it better or get it going again! These men and women not only use these skillsets on the job (in!), but I've watched them also use these very same abilities to serve individuals, families, and groups both locally and globally (through!). In and through. Got it?

Let me throw something out there and then ask you a question.

Most people who I know operate in their vocations solely on what they have learned from their educational experiences, things they've added from books or online, or have maybe been taught by a friend. And, that's great! However, with that said, the vast majority of followers of Jesus who I know have _never_ been deliberately discipled to think, relate, or work within their vocations with God's character, ways, and mission in mind—or have even once considered making disciples of Jesus in their vocation!

Have you?

Imagine with me, how vocational disciple making could transform how a government leader governs; a medical professional serves; a scientist observes and measures; and how a business leader treats their employees and customers! How differently might the world look if the godly parent, educator, artist/musician, athlete, news anchor, techie, farmer, disaster relief worker, and cause-driven activist carried within them the character, ways, and mission of Jesus!

Consider for a moment your own current work environment.

- How different might it be if those leading you were discipled around the character of God and led based on His ways?
- What impact would it make if your boss expressed genuine interest and care for the people who work for them?
- What if your fellow workers got to work on time, finished tasks better than ever, and had great attitudes because they know Whom it is they ultimately serve?
- What if the "bottom line" wasn't money, position, or promotion, but instead was to make sure that every customer/member/client was treated honorably and served in such a way that their needs were met?
- How much of an impact could be made in your community or around the world if the skill sets contained within fellow followers of Jesus whom you work with were unleashed to advance His mission and better and bless the lives of others?

Imagine the ramifications for a company, a community, a country if we determined to deliberately vocationally disciple followers of Jesus! Jesus knows the transforming power it holds for people, families, and entire societies!

Calling and Co-Missioning. Vocation and Disciple Making.

Connecting the two is imperative in the world we are living in today.

This is the great opportunity!

AIMING FOR APPLICATION

1. How did you get into your current vocation? Did you see God's hand on it? If so, how?

2. As a disciple of Jesus, what are you actively doing to participate in the Great Co-Mission?

3. Have you ever connected your vocation with disciple making? Why or why not?

CHAPTER 2

A Polished Arrow

While giving leadership to a youth discipleship camp some years ago, I met Kirk, a young man who had just agreed to come on board as the youth pastor of a recent church plant. Our camp was a good place for him to bond and hang for a week with the teens that he was about to pastor for the next season of his life. We quickly hit it off through common interests and mutual hearts of investing in the next generation. Kirk and his wife, Brooke, were people who both my wife, Cheryl, and I enjoyed being with, and we were honored to be invited to pour the ways of God into them.

About eight years into our relationship, I was doing some speaking for them and, per usual, Kirk and I grabbed some time together. One morning, while having breakfast at a local restaurant, he began to share his heart with me about the possibility of changing his vocation. He felt like the Lord was stirring something in his heart about moving more toward business to make an impact in the marketplace. I remember thinking that Kirk was entrepreneurial enough, great with people, and had a skill set that would translate well, so I didn't have any difficulty seeing this as a possibility.

After listening to Kirk and Brooke share their hearts, he asked me what I thought. I affirmed to him what I had been thinking and added what I knew needed to be the centerpiece of this process. I said, "The question here is not do you have the ability to change vocations—because you certainly do. The question is, are you walking in obedience to Jesus in both direction and timing—and is He done shaping your character and skills where He has you now?"

As a couple who was committed to living as disciples of Jesus, Kirk and Brooke already knew the prominent place of obedience to Jesus in all areas of their lives. It was my role that day to simply keep that in front of them. I also knew that in one's twenties and thirties, it's always more about what God is building within them than what He is pouring through them. I was aware that if they stepped out too soon, they could short circuit the shaping process of God in their lives. I challenged them to create an "altar point," a place to lay their next steps before the Lord, allowing Him to lead and guide them.

As they wrestled with this decision and sought the Lord in the weeks ahead, they recognized the timing wasn't right and that God was indeed not done shaping them more around His character and ways in the setting He currently had them in. As a matter of fact, in obedience to Jesus, they stayed put for another four years, with some of those years not being easy! They chose to trust the Lord, who always sees the big picture and added much to their lives that they would benefit from and draw upon later.

Sure enough, after those four years, the Lord led them to a new vocation of business. The stirring of Kirk's heart years prior had been exactly right! He saw Jesus and glimpses of his future, but in obedience to Jesus "stayed put" until He was done using his current setting to shape him more around God's character and ways. Waiting to be sent in God's timing has led to blessing, fruitfulness, and favor in business. Looking back on their journey, Kirk and Brooke see God's hand in both their obedience and His shaping process to prepare their lives for His greater purposes!

*****

Calling.

In the Scriptures, we find God calling people to participate with Him in His purposes. He invites them to join Him in reconciling relationships and redeeming lives, turning people's worlds from floundering to flourishing! He puts His hand on the life of a man or a woman and shapes them into an arrow—a polished arrow—in His hands.

> *The Lord called me from the womb, from the body of my mother he named my name. He made my mouth like a sharp sword; in the shadow of his hand he hid me; he made me a polished arrow; in his quiver he hid me away. And he said to me, "You are my servant, Israel, in whom I will be glorified." (Isaiah 49:1–3)*

The Lord "called" Isaiah from the womb, naming Him, making his mouth like a sharp sword and his life like a polished arrow for His purposes.

*Before I formed you in the womb I knew you, and before you were
born I consecrated you; I appointed you a prophet to the nations.*
(Jeremiah 1:5)

Here, we see Jeremiah being appointed a prophet to the nations
before being formed in the womb!

When we consider John the Baptist, the forerunner of Jesus,
the Scriptures state:

*...he will be filled with the Holy Spirit, even from his mother's
womb. And he will turn many of the children of Israel to the Lord
their God, and he will go before him in the spirit and power of
Elijah, to turn the hearts of the fathers to the children, and the
disobedient to the wisdom of the just, to make ready for the Lord a
people prepared.* (Luke 1:15–17)

Consider what this is saying, not only about John, but about
our lives. God has dreams about what He desires to do in and
through us long before our very first breath!

In Psalm 139, David provides us with a little glimpse of God's
activity while we are in our mother's womb:

*For you formed my inward parts; you knitted me together in my
mother's womb. I praise you, for I am fearfully and wonderfully
made. Wonderful are your works; my soul knows it very well. Your
eyes saw my unformed substance; in your book were written, every
one of them, the days that were formed for me, when as yet there
was none of them.* (Psalm 139:13–14, 16)

He formed you, knitted you together, and had things in mind
for you before your very first day! Think of the joy in the heart of

your Heavenly Father as He's fashioning you: seeing what you'll look like when you're all grown up; placing wonderful abilities, skills, and gifts within you; and envisioning the unique role in His Kingdom that only you will play to fulfill His purposes!

I love what the Scriptures go on to say about David,

For David, after he had served the purpose of God in his own generation, fell asleep and was laid with his fathers... (Acts 13:36)

Serving the purpose of God in one's own generation—now that is what we're after!

Purpose with generational impact.

That is a conversation that often emerges with people I interact with, men and women of all ages and seasons of life. Because God has made each of us with a divine purpose, until we hit that mark we can find ourselves wondering and wandering through life.

I've found that sometimes a person is using their God-given natural abilities or spiritual gifts in the right way, but in a setting that is not the right fit for them. I've watched others go from job to job, focusing only on pay, and when finally finding the paycheck they wanted, realize they don't really like what they are doing with that forty to fifty hours each week. And then there are those precious twenty- and thirty-somethings in my life, whom I greatly love. They often are caught attempting to find their vocational "stride" when God is using their current work world to mold their characters and grow their competencies for greater Kingdom purposes that He has in mind for them later in life's journey.

Over the last four-plus decades, I've observed a Scriptural process about calling that I'd like to share with you in a more devotional, reflective kind of way. It may strike you a little different than how you've considering calling in the past. However, if you are open to it, it has great possibilities of aligning you to God's ways of discovering, developing, and deploying you toward your calling and God's purposes.

Seeing—Shaping—Sending

Moments ago, we viewed the passage in Isaiah 49 about Isaiah being a polished arrow in God's hand. Many years earlier, in Isaiah 6, before becoming that polished arrow, we read about this incredible experience in Isaiah's life.

> *In the year that King Uzziah died I saw the Lord sitting upon a throne, high and lifted up; and the train of his robe filled the temple. Above him stood the seraphim. Each had six wings: with two he covered his face, and with two he covered his feet, and with two he flew. And one called to another and said:*
>
> *"Holy, holy, holy is the Lord of hosts; the whole earth is full of his glory!"*
>
> *And the foundations of the thresholds shook at the voice of him who called, and the house was filled with smoke. And I said: "Woe is me! For I am lost; for I am a man of unclean lips, and I dwell in the midst of a people of unclean lips; for my eyes have seen the King, the Lord of hosts!"*
>
> *Then one of the seraphim flew to me, having in his hand a burning coal that he had taken with tongs from the altar. And he touched my mouth and said: "Behold, this has touched your lips; your guilt is taken away, and your sin atoned for."*
>
> *And I heard the voice of the Lord saying, "Whom shall I send, and who will go for us?" Then I said, "Here I am! Send me."* (Isaiah 6:1–8)

I'd like for you to note the progression here.

First, there is an *upward look*, where Isaiah sees the King, the Lord of hosts, on His throne, and hears the heavenly refrain of "holy, holy, holy" coming from those surrounding Him.

Second, this wonderfully terrifying sight moves Isaiah to an *inward look*, leading toward inner transformation and preparation for God's call on his life.

And third, there comes an *outward look*, with Isaiah's heart now rightly aligned, he hears the voice of God calling and makes himself available to the service of His King.

Isaiah's seeing God leads to his shaping by God, resulting in sending from God.

This is God's ways when it comes to calling. You'll see this pattern throughout Scripture in the lives of the godly men and women you've read about and admired.

I have found that, way too often, we look first at the sending part, walking lightly on the seeing God part, while rushing as fast as we can through the shaping part. Sending without seeing and shaping often results in an overall "spiritual thinness," character and relational issues that tend to mark our lives, and not referencing God's Kingdom purposes through our lives and vocations.

Each of these three pieces from Isaiah's story—seeing, shaping, and sending—play vital roles in becoming the "polished arrow" that fulfills the calling of God on our lives.

Seeing

When considering calling, and Isaiah's encounter, it all begins with seeing God.

Picture this. Isaiah sees the Lord sitting upon a throne, high and lifted up. Six-winged beings, called seraphim, call to one another,

Holy, holy, holy is the Lord of hosts; the whole earth is full of his glory! The foundations of the thresholds are shaking at His voice. Smoke fills the house. Seeing God—experiencing His presence, encountering His character, and hearing His voice—leaves Isaiah completely undone! Never again will he be the same.

Gazing at God does that to a woman and a man.

It ruins them for anything and everything ordinary.

It recalibrates not only how they view God, but how they see and do life.

God's presence, His character, His voice. Friendship with God first!

How have you experienced God's presence? You know, that wonderful sense of both awe and nearness. Maybe in that quiet place of prayer. Or, while reflecting on His truth in the Scriptures. Could be while you are worshipping at home or among fellow followers of Jesus. During a season of fasting. Or, possibly on a walk in the woods or on the beach where you are pouring out your heart to your Heavenly Father or just enjoying being with Him.

We are to be a people of His presence. It's what distinguishes followers of Jesus from all other people on the planet! Moses recognized this in Exodus 33:16,

> *Is it not in your going with us, so that we are distinct, I and your people, from every other people on the face of the earth?*

Are you pursuing God's presence, making place for it in your daily life? If not, why not?

What about encountering God's character? Do you see Him in such a way that you can love Him, trust Him completely, and be fully dependent upon Him?

Understand, the enemy of your soul, the devil, has been busy since the beginning of your life doing all he can to distort and disfigure God's character in your heart and mind. He knows if you see God for who He really is, as revealed in the Scriptures, you'll be forever transformed!

One of the ways I've experienced God's character more is by highlighting every name, title, and attribute of His character in my Bible with a purple pencil. It's a powerful thing to allow God to show you for Himself, through the Scriptures, what He is really like! This continues to replace false impressions that I had believed about Him from what others, the devil, or life itself had imprinted upon my soul. This has grown my love for and trust in God, as well as my worship life, and leaning on Him while following His lead via daily obedience.

What is the most current aspect of who He is that He's been revealing to you? Are you leaning into it for more?

Isaiah also heard God's voice, becoming attuned to it so when the call came, He could respond.

The Scriptures teach us in John 10 that as His sheep, we can hear our Shepherd's voice. I don't know about you, but I've never heard the audible voice of God. I have, however, over the years learned to discern—through both success and failure—when God is trying to say something or lead me. He uses the Scriptures, prayer, and waiting on Him. He also often guides me through an abiding kind of peace, life circumstances, and the people He has placed in my life. Occasionally, there are more supernatural kinds of expressions as well, like dreams or prophetic words from others that point me to what He is saying.

When was the last time you paused to give ear to hearing God's voice? He longs to speak to you about His love and relationship with you, as well as how He wants to lead and guide you.

For Isaiah, seeing God meant experiencing His presence, encountering His character, and hearing His voice. Friendship with God at the forefront. I have found over the years, walking alongside many in various places and vocations, that it's truly where calling begins.

Shaping

When seeing God, it revealed a place in Isaiah's life where He needed God to transform Him. It had to do with his mouth, *for I am a man of unclean lips, and I dwell in the midst of a people of unclean lips.* In this passage, we see the goodness and graciousness of the Lord touching his mouth and making him clean. It is interesting to me that considering Isaiah's calling to be a prophetic voice, one of the things that needed shaping was his mouth!

To help us here, I'd like to reference the "polished arrow" and the process of shaping a twig into one.

In the Hebrew language of the Old Testament, the word "polished" means *to select, choose, purify, polish, purge, cleanse, make bright, test or prove.*

When selecting a twig to transform, the arrow maker sees beyond the twig's present form to what it can become when shaped in his hands. He may need to trim it, sand it, eliminate knots, possibly dry it out, and put it through the fire before it is ready to be polished. All this is meticulously and deliberately done so that the arrow will be proven and tested, rightly fitted in both bow and the archer's hand, and fly true to hit its mark!

Knowing the challenges ahead of you, your Heavenly Father loves you so much that He won't send you into the full stride of your calling until He has first shaped you for it!

Like the shaft of an arrow, He knows where you need to be trimmed and what aspects of your character need some smoothing through sanding. He'll use your relationships and vocation to work out the knots and will put you through the fire of challenging circumstances. He'll heal and redeem you and free you from those stuck places of the soul. He'll equip you with every good gift that you'll need. He does all this so when it's time to hit your stride you will be tested and proven, rightly fitted within His hand, and ready to be flung far for His purposes.

Many years ago, while sitting under the tutelage of Dr. Bobby Clinton[1], I learned that God's character shaping continues throughout our entire lives but is especially prominent while in our twenties and thirties. As a matter of fact, when I have the privilege of relating to, teaching, and discipling men and women of that age, they hear me say, "Always remember, in your twenties and thirties, it is more important what God is building in you than what He is doing through you."

According to Dr. Clinton's years of extensive research on godly leaders, a person doesn't usually hit the full stride of their calling until they are into their fifties or even their early sixties. It is in that season of life where seasoned and tested character meets the mature use of one's gifts, and a God-determined sphere of influence emerges. Considering that it took Moses two-thirds of his life to be prepared for his calling (80 of his 120 years), and Jesus 10/11 of his (30 of 33 years), this provides us with some fresh perspective and a new paradigm to look through as it relates to calling.

As a twenty-year-old missionary, I remember Loren Cunningham, YWAM's founder and one of the key disciple makers in my life, saying to me, "the broader the calling, the longer the preparation." We need to fully embrace and trust God's shaping process within us.

So, don't rush it, trust it!

Allow the shaping of God to have its full way in you. He knows when you are ready. He also knows when it's time for your sending, and He'll open doors for you that no one can shut!

Sending

It's only after Isaiah sees God, and is shaped by Him, that sending happens. Isaiah became an effective prophetic voice in God's hands to Israel, Judah, and other nations. He and his family were also used by God as signs and wonders in Israel (Isaiah 8:18). His mouth was used mightily to prophecy about the future coming of Jesus, the Messiah, and His Kingdom. Jewish tradition tells us that Isaiah's life came to an end when he was killed by being sawn in two. When looking at the whole of Isaiah's life, we can see why the "seeing and shaping" was of utmost importance before God's "sending."

Calling is about God sending us into society where He wants us to represent Him. It is a holy thing. It is never about just running off to "do something for God" or "using my gifts" and asking God to bless us. Rather, God is always the initiator, the one who "sets our target": a person or people needing to be served; an organization that must be built; a mission or task that needs to be accomplished; a certain group of people or area of society impacted, etc.

As we'll see a bit later, embedded within calling—regardless of what God calls one to do—are three scriptural reference points: God's Kingdom being advanced, the lives of people around us being bettered and blessed, and His name glorified. Without these, we must question whether we are fulfilling the calling of God on our lives or simply "going to work"!

We live in a culture and era of time where much of our identity, focus and pursuit is on "what I do." Neglecting the "seeing and shaping by God" process, can hinder what God desires to express through us when it comes time to hitting our calling stride. However, if we align ourselves to God's calling process, He *is able to do far more abundantly than all that we ask or think, according to the power at work within us...*! (Ephesians 3:20)

When it comes to the components of one's calling, it looks a bit like a math equation to me:

Passion + Giftedness + Vocational Field +
Opportunity + Obedience

<u>Passion</u> is the part of us that expresses our deepest desires and drives. It can cause both excitement and motivation, enabling us to sacrifice much to accomplish our purpose.

Here are a few of the many questions I ask people to begin to help them sort out what really is tucked deeply within their hearts:

If you knew you would absolutely succeed, what need in the world would you meet?

What do you enjoy doing most for others?

If you could have anyone's job and flourish in it, whose would it be and why?

Is there a group of people, mission or task that your heart consistently returns to?

For what would you be willing to endure hardships, even be persecuted for?

At the end of your life, where would you like to know that you made a difference?

How did you answer those? You may need a long walk on the beach or up in the mountains in the woods to grapple with these kinds of questions. Don't be afraid of that, it's a good wrestling!

<u>Giftedness</u>, in my mind, is a blend of three things: your natural abilities, acquired skills, and spiritual gifts. *Natural abilities* are

talents and aptitudes that come easy to you, likely since childhood, while acquired skills are things learned from others along the way. *Spiritual gifts* are those unique supernatural capacities deposited by the Holy Spirit that express God's love and power through your life. All three are given by God and need to be referenced when speaking of one's overall gift package. In my own experience, any one of the three can serve as a person's primary expression with the other two enhancing and complementing it.

Vocational Field represents where God has appointed you to serve in society, usually some 40–50 hours per week. We'll take a much greater look at this in upcoming chapters.

Opportunity speaks of doors that God opens for you to step through to accomplish His Kingdom purposes. Many times, opportunity has to do with meeting a need of a person, a family, a community or even an entire nation. During our lifetimes, God presents us with various opportunities that we need to seek His face about. It's important to note here that not every "open door" is a door you are to walk through, nor is every "closed door" a door you are to walk away from. Many a missionary has walked into "closed nations" to bring the Gospel because Jesus asked them to go. Which brings us to our last part of this calling equation.

Obedience, which is intended to be learned and practiced on the front end in the "seeing and shaping by God" parts of the process, plays an important role when it comes to "sending."

Just because there is a need or opportunity before you does not necessarily mean you are to rush right into it. (Of course, if your neighbor's toilet is overflowing and water is gushing out the front door, you should be over there helping them, not praying about it… just hear me out…) Jesus was certainly deeply touched by human need. However, *Jesus was not driven by needs but rather was led by obedience.* A read-through of the story of Lazarus in

John 11 reveals that afresh to us. You want to be doing what you're doing because you know that God has led you there, not just because it's a good idea. Walking in obedience keeps us tethered to friendship with God, to seeking Him first, and walking in a humble confidence that He has placed us where He's got us.

His Polished Arrow

Consider the lengths and breadths that God goes to when it comes to us being prepared for His calling on our lives. He passionately pursues us so that the foundation of our calling is intimate friendship with Himself, *seeing* Him for who He really is so we can both enjoy and trust Him. He invests massive amounts of time and sovereignly orchestrates the events of our lives and the people He places on our paths to redeem us from inner stuck places while deliberately *shaping* our character for His purposes. Then, He stirs us by allowing us to experience a little of His heart for someone or something that is important to Him, all while incredibly outfitting us with the gift package we'll need as He pulls back His bow, *sending* us as His polished arrow to represent Him in a world that desperately needs Him.

God. Calling. Seeing. Shaping. Sending.

Amazing!

AIMING FOR APPLICATION

1. Reflecting on the most impacting encounter(s) you've had with God, what did He reveal to you about Himself? How did you see Him differently from that point on?

2. How is God using the current circumstances of your life to shape your character to be more like and reflective of His?

3. Where has/is God sending you as a polished arrow to serve on His behalf in society?

CHAPTER 3

A Vocational Vantage Point

In March of 1976, while in my junior year of high school, I made my first trip to Kona, on the Big Island of Hawai'i. My dad and a dear friend of his had accepted an invitation to participate in a month-long YWAM leadership seminar. During their seminar, my mom, dad, brother, and I, along with Dad's friend and his family, made the trip to the beautiful Aloha State.

While enjoying the hospitality of the Polynesian people, the scenic beaches, the tropical scents, and the tastes of the "local grindz," we took in a session or two with Dad. Following one of them, I met and was challenged by Loren Cunningham to come to the Discipleship Training School (DTS) after I graduated the following year. At that point in time, I was planning to attend the

University of Minnesota's School of Journalism, aiming for a career in television broadcasting. How little did I realize that Jesus had another plan for my life on His heart!

Halfway through my senior year, I applied to the U of M and to the DTS in Kona. I was accepted at both! Through prayer, and the counsel of my parents and others, I decided to go where I felt the Lord was leading—back to Kona to attend the DTS!

As I began DTS in September of 1977, we were asked to choose groups based around vocational fields. These were small groups focused around the family, the church, government, education, media, arts/entertainment, and business. Of course, with where I believed I was headed at the time, I chose the media group.

We met twice a week to intercede for leaders in that area of society, learn more about it, and prayerfully consider strategies the Lord might share with us to impact that field. As an eighteen-year-old, I was gaining a whole new vantage point. It began to shape how I viewed the world around me, including calling and vocation. Whether I would become a television broadcaster, go on to be a missionary, or pursue another vocation, I realized I could actively participate in advancing God's Kingdom wherever He appointed me to serve within society.

What I didn't realize at the time was how this thinking had come about. In the summer of 1975, Loren and his wife, Darlene, were taking a little time away in Colorado. While there, the Lord impressed on Loren a new thought he'd never considered before—that nations can be reached through impacting their various spheres of influence.

At this same time, Loren and Darlene received an invitation to visit with Bill and Vonette Bright, founders of Campus Crusade for Christ, who were also visiting Colorado. As they began comparing what the Lord had been sharing with them, they were amazed to find that Jesus had been putting in their hearts essentially the same list of spheres of influence! As additional confirmation to where the Lord was leading, Darlene heard Dr. Francis Schaeffer articulating a similar set of society shapers shortly after the Cunninghams and Brights had met. They knew God was up to something!

Two years later, this understanding was making quite an impression on me as I participated as a student in the DTS in Kona. It provided me with a strategic way to see and pray for our nation and the world. It allowed me to view the value of each person's unique calling through the vocations within society. I saw how people could be treated honorably and effectively served through each vocation, thus glorifying God. Most significantly, it offered what would become a lifelong framework for me to view vocations through the lens of disciple making.

*****

A long as I can remember, there has been a perceived gulf between those in "secular jobs" and those in "the ministry." Ministry folks appeared to be more sacrificial and spiritual, while those working in the secular realm were perceived to be a little less holy and often "caught up in the things of the world." I'm grateful this kind of thinking is not on the radar of the current generation that is being raised up. Instead, they want to know how their vocation is tied to the Kingdom of God!

Consider these words from German priest, professor, and Reformation leader, Martin Luther: "The idea that service to God should have only to do with the church altar, singing, reading, sacrifice, and the like is without doubt but the worst trick of the devil. How could the devil have led us more effectively astray than by the narrow conception that service to God takes place only in church and by works done therein... The whole world could abound with services to the Lord... not only in churches but also in home, kitchen, workshop, field."[1]

Through the process of my own discipleship, I learned in Scripture that there really is no such thing as "the sacred" and "the secular." Psalm 24:1 reminds us, "The earth is the Lord's and the fullness thereof, the world and those who dwell therein." John 1:3 affirms the same, "All things were made through Him, and without Him was not any thing made that was made."

I really like what Pastor Jack Hayford says about this in Lionshare's *Fathers of the Faith* video series, "The division in the mind of God is not between the sacred arena and a secular arena. But the division is between the light and the dark. There's darkness across the face of the Earth, and the Lord wants to seed it all with the sons and daughters of light."[2]

Walking as disciples of Jesus means every area of our lives has been yielded to His Lordship, including what we do to get paid during a certain forty to fifty hours each week. Many view what they do during those hours as a way to put bread on the table so they can do what they really want to do. However, I'd submit there's another vocational vantage point!

As you'll remember, the root of the English word "vocation" is the Latin word *vocatio*, which means "calling." Martin Luther believed that having a vocation is more than simply an occupation; rather, it encompasses the whole life of the follower of Jesus and is not limited to job, career, trade, or profession. He believed one's vocation was a calling for followers of Jesus to contribute to the world around them by serving others.

Luther wrote, "A cobbler, a smith, a farmer, each has the work and office of his trade, and yet they are all alike consecrated priests and bishops, and every one by means of his own work or office must benefit and serve every other, that in this way many kinds of work may be done for the bodily and spiritual welfare of the community, even as all the members of the body serve one another."[3]

The term "vocation" had long been used to describe "sacred" ministry and the religious orders. Luther seems to be the first to use "vocation" to refer also to "secular" offices and occupations. Today, the term has become common, another synonym for our profession or job. But behind the term is the notion that every legitimate kind of work or social function is a distinct "calling" from God, requiring unique God-given gifts, skills, and talents. Moreover, the Reformation doctrine of vocation teaches that God himself is active in everyday human labor, family responsibilities, and social interactions.

God created each of us to play a unique and meaningful role in society. He intended that we be linked by love, serving one another out of friendship while always benefiting the community at large. As each one serves through his God-given measures of capacity and influence, people are taken care of and real needs are met. William Perkins, the only Puritan author to describe callings in a systematic way, emphasized calling as "a certain kind of life ordained and imposed on man by God, for the common good."

One of Luther's examples, enhanced by Gene Edward Veith, helps us better understand the value and integration of our vocations: "We pray in the Lord's Prayer that God give us our daily bread, which He does. He does so, not directly as when he gave manna to the Israelites, but through the work of farmers and bakers—and we might add truck drivers and retailers."

"In effect, the whole economic system is the means by which God gives us our daily bread. Each part of the economic food chain is a *vocation*, through which God works to distribute his gifts."

"Similarly, God heals the sick. While He can and sometimes does do so directly, in the normal course of things He works through doctors, nurses, and other medical experts. God protects us from evil, with the vocation of the police officer. God teaches through teachers, orders society through governments, proclaims the Gospel through pastors. Luther pointed out that God could populate the earth by creating each new generation of babies from the dust. Instead, He ordained that human beings should come together to bring up children in families. The offices of husband, wife, and parent are *vocations* through which God works to rear and care for children."[4]

Veith continues, "God is graciously at work, caring for the human race through the work of other human beings. Behind the care we have received from our parents, the education we received from our teachers, the benefits we receive from our spouse, our employers, and our government stands God himself, bestowing His blessings."

"The picture is of a vast, complex society of human beings with different talents and abilities. Each serves the other; each is served by others. We Americans have an ideal of self-sufficiency and often dream of being able to grow our own food, build our own homes, and live independently of other people. But our proper human condition is *dependence*. Because of the centrality of love, we are to depend on other human beings and, ultimately and through them, on God. Conversely, other people are to depend on us. In God's earthly Kingdom, we are to receive His blessings from other people in their vocations."

"The purpose of one's vocation, whatever it might be, is serving others. It has to do with fulfilling Christ's injunction to love one's neighbor. Though justification has nothing to do with good works, vocation does involve good works. The Christian's relationship to God is based on sheer grace and forgiveness on God's part; the Christian's relationship to other people, however, is to be based on love. As [Gustaf] Wingren puts it, 'God does not need our good works, but our neighbor does.'"[5]

In framing vocations, Luther talked about them as the "masks of God," since God is actually the one at work behind what He's appointed us to do: "All our work in the field, in the garden, in the city, in the home, in struggle, in government—to what does it all amount before God except child's play, by means of which God is pleased to give His gifts in the field, at home, and everywhere? These are the masks of our Lord God, behind which He wants to be hidden and to do all things."[6] Luther's thinking leads to his characterization that "God Himself is milking the cows through the vocation of the milkmaid."[7]

For some, I am describing things here that fortify what you already understand about calling and vocation. For others, this may be introducing fresh thoughts that will invigorate you as you view your life and vocation from this point forward.

Vocations: Rooted in the Character of God

As I began to come alongside leaders and people serving in various vocations, I observed a couple of things about vocational fields. First, these various expressions of calling and service are not just good ideas or nice things to be able to do for a living. Eternally, they have significantly more value than that, as they are rooted in God Himself! That's right, these vocational fields are expressions of the character of the God we love, worship, and serve. This understanding provides us with a whole different way of looking at and approaching what it is each of us is called to do.

Let me illustrate what I mean.

Today, I can get off a plane and turn on the device in my hand to receive, instantaneously, every message conceivable, from voicemail to text to email to social media. I am completely baffled as to how all this information is available at my fingertips. But, as I experience it, I am given the tiniest glimpse of the power of God's processing ability. I am reminded that He knows the past, present, and future and is alert to what's going on in the entire physical and spiritual realm at any given time. I am amazed that He is attentive to every single molecule and aware of the location of every person on the planet, conscious of the positioning of the seventy-nine moons of Jupiter and knowledgeable of the deepest secrets of every heart—all at the same time! When I look at Jesus as the one behind the vocation of technology, I stand in wonder and awe, worshipping Him in a way I had not previously considered.

What about Jesus, the Author of creation? The human body contains some 60,000 miles of blood vessels. If laid out in a single row, they would wrap around the earth some two-and-a-half times! What about the sun? Did you know that the sun is approximately 109 times the diameter of the earth and can fit more than one million Earths inside of it? Mind-boggling! God also created the earth just the right distance from the sun. If it were further away, we'd freeze. If it were closer, we'd all burn up! What about this thing we call water that makes up approximately 60% of our physical beings and around 72% of Earth's surface? No living thing on the planet can survive without it! What amazing stuff—and what an amazing God, who is behind environmental and scientific vocations!

Early morning sunrises on the beaches of Hawaii reveal the canvas of God. It begins with flashes of first light turning darkness into dawn with the morning clouds momentarily reflecting daybreak colors. Then, the sun begins its slow, majestic rise to reign daily over the vibrant blue Pacific waters. Welcome to the work of God the Artist! Think about the many other works that have originated from His heavenly hands—the perfect spots on the back of a ladybug, the flawless form of a rose, the grandeur of the giant sequoia, the bright and bold expressions of the sunflower, and the uniqueness of each snowflake.

Have you considered God the Master Builder? When Noah was asked to build the ark, God provided him with detailed dimensions. It was to be made of gopher wood, and it was to be 300 cubits long, 50 cubits wide, and 30 cubits high. Depending on whether the cubits of measurement were the typical 17.5 inches or the Egyptian royal cubit of 20.5 inches, it means the ark was 437 or 512 feet in length! With these measurements, there would have been over 100,000 square feet of floor space[8]—just what would have been needed for Noah's family and his thousands of paired creatures! The same kind of instruction and detail goes into the building of the Tabernacle and everything contained within it, including the Ark of the Covenant. Builders, your calling is rooted in God Himself!

As we watch governments collapse before our very eyes, I am grateful that we belong to an everlasting Kingdom! The King of this Kingdom governs with abundant mercy, consistent justice, and benevolence born of His own sacrifice. His subjects are never His slaves but rather His friends. His vision is such that the wealthy want to give generously, and the poor are provided with opportunities to grow so both can give their lives in service for others!

I think you get my point. The vocations aren't just places where we work and get paid. They are meant to reflect and display various aspects of God's character through our lives as we do what we do. It's a very practical way for each of us to bring glory to God!

Vocational DNA

I've also noticed that each vocational field seems to have its own distinct "strands of DNA." Defining these helps determine each vocation's unique value and function, and results in improved goods or services produced, which betters the lives of others. These strands represent God's thumbprint on that vocational field. Through them, God can be glorified, people can be honored, and real needs can be met.

First, each vocational field contains a God-given <u>competence</u> that can be used to serve others. Of course, abilities, skills, and gifts overlap the vocations; yet, each field has a certain contribution through which it can specifically serve others. For example:

- *Those serving within the field of technology can use their unique competence to resource, train, and fix our gadgets.*
- *Those leading a disaster relief service organization can use their competence to help people navigate their way through the challenge of losing property and loved ones.*

Second, each vocational field develops and/or makes available <u>distinct products and/or specific services</u> to meet the needs of others. Each vocational field shares with its community, or the rest of the world, their work for the betterment of society. For example:

- *Those working in the field that deals with fuel meet the needs of energy for people's homes, vehicles, and work.*
- *Those working in the vocational field of media provide information for the public that can aid in understanding, making choices, and even the saving of lives.*

Third, each vocational field has a unique range of <u>impact</u>. With some fields, the influence is broad and expansive. With others, it may be narrow and focused. For example:

- *Those serving in the field of arts/entertainment/sports can make an impact through their performance on a huge amount of people.*
- *Those serving in education as home schooling parents make an impact on their own children.*

Fourth, each vocational field contains relationships to enjoy and team together with. The like-heartedness that comes from working together creates lifelong friendships and an ease in partnering together on tasks. For example:

- *Those serving in the field of professional team sports understand that team unity is one of the keys to winning championships.*
- *Those serving in the field of surgical medicine recognize that a patient's health or life depends on that surgical team working well together.*

Fifth, and finally, each vocational field has a specialized mission to be accomplished on behalf of others. The aims of each field may be different, yet each one is used to meet the real needs of people. Like everything else in the Kingdom of God, as each one serves the other, every need is met. For example:

- *Those serving within government are meant to create and enforce laws that benefit their society and protect its people.*
- *Those serving in the Church are to create an environment where people can experience God, walk in community, grow as disciples, and impact others locally and globally.*

Luther's insights.

The Character of God.

Vocational DNA.

These kinds of vantage points allow us to see more clearly what we do day-in-and-day-out through the lens of the Lord. They reveal afresh the holiness or "set apartness" of our lives. My friend, it's not "just a job" you go do, it's doing God's work everywhere you go! It's not a "profession," rather, its partnering with God in His purposes. And it's certainly not your "career," but rather a calling to see "Thy Kingdom come, Thy will be done, on Earth as it is in heaven"!

AIMING FOR APPLICATION

1. What did you learn from Luther about calling and vocation?

2. How does God uniquely desire to express His character through your vocation?

3. Considering the five strands of vocational DNA above, how do those apply to your vocation?

CHAPTER 4

Vocational Fields of Service

Several decades ago, while visiting a good friend who was planting a church, I met one of his new members. While chatting together, I learned that Harrison was a cardiologist, and from what others were telling me, he was maybe one of the best in his field. Along with doing his own job, he was often sought after by others in and around his field to provide counsel on how to do their jobs better.

As the years passed, Harrison and I have become good friends. His wife, Hope, is dear to both my wife and me, their kids participated with our kids in our annual youth discipleship camps, and we've supported and cheered each other on as we've all tried to obey Jesus in the fields where He has appointed each of us to serve.

Over time, he shared his heart and life with me. Like many in his vocation, Harrison is extremely smart, incredibly capable, and maybe even too gifted for one person! He is also very focused and locked in on whatever is in front of him. (That seems like a great attribute to me when working on someone whose chest is opened and heart needs help!) This man always gets the job done and done well. He is someone you can count on to get the task done, no matter what he is asked or volunteers to do.

One day, as we were talking, he shared with me that he'd often overrun people to get the task in front of him done. The Lord had been speaking to him about this, and the fact that he was concerned about it revealed to me where the Holy Spirit was working in his life.

Walking together over the years, enjoying friendship, and talking about God's ways, I had observed that tucked inside of Harrison was a genuine and deep love and care for people. He cared for others in a way that was both sacrificial and generous. However, at times, relationships could be challenging because of his constant focus on tasks. He expressed how he desired for this to change.

Because of his hunger for the truth of Scripture and his humility, he was open to learn and grow. And grow he did! As I watched him attack the ways of God regarding relating well with the same focus as he took on his tasks, I watched the Spirit of God work within him! Today, not only is Harrison good in his vocational craft, but he has grown as a better relater—and as he'd tell you, continues to grow! He now expresses God's love and care well to his patients, those he works with, and within the relationships he enjoys throughout his life. He also deliberately reproduces what he's learned of God's ways to those in his relational spheres and within his vocation.

If you happen to be making the rounds in the hospital with Harrison, not only would you see him giving his patients an update on the medical condition of their heart, but you'd also see him sitting down to talk and pray with them about the real cares and concerns of their spiritual heart!

*****

So, what vocational field(s) has God appointed you to serve within? You are there to be His ambassador to advance His Kingdom, better and bless the lives of people, and glorify His name.

Granted, you may not yet have landed in the role that allows you to hit the stride of your calling, as He may be using your current role more for shaping you for His purposes later in life (think Isaiah 6: seeing—shaping—sending). It's in these times that you want to ask God questions like: "What are You trying to form and develop within me?"

Looking through these kinds of lenses allows your spiritual and vocational muscles to grow, and develops godly habits of thinking, attitudes of heart, and actions to take, thus preparing you for where God wants you to serve down the road!

Building on the vantage points of the last chapter, I want to provide you with a lineup of vocational fields that leaders I walk with reference. It's not intended as a "be all, end all" list, but rather a reference point for recognizing your vocational calling so you can be more intentional in participating with God's ways and purposes in it.

I understand that you may find yourself actively engaged in several of these fields—and that's great! I also realize that these vocational fields often overlap with each other. For example, the field of Agriculture might represent the source of food, while the field of (Culinary) Arts focuses on the food's presentation, and it's through the field of Business that food arrives into the hands of the consumer. The fields of Arts & Entertainment, Media, and Technology interface often these days. The field of Family shapes the lives of our children and teenagers, as does the fields of Education and the Church—not to mention the three we just previously stated! Key service industries that are often tied to business, like waiting tables, skin care, haircutting, housecleaning, janitorial services, landscaping, tax prep and automotive care, may also overlap vocational fields. You get the picture.

So, let's jump in, taking a brief peek at these various vocational fields of service, referencing a Kingdom perspective for each one, and briefly identifying how each is rooted in the character of God.

The Family

After getting the Garden of Eden ready, God created a family. He brought Eve to Adam, joining man and woman in marriage, and along came children that needed to be cared for and shaped by a father and a mother. Soon enough, siblings, aunties and uncles, cousins, nieces and nephews, and grandparents were added to the mix, each contributing to the joys and journey of family life.

Families are the foundation of every single culture on the planet and are its centerpiece of life. God's intention is that the family would provide meaningful relationships, nurturing, and godly modeling as we grow and develop, providing a safe environment to experience and share life through unconditional love.

While every couple and parent is to prioritize their family, for some, family is their vocational calling. For example, consider the vital role of the homemaker, which is fast becoming a lost art! Or, the homeschooler, committed to faithfully educating their children. What about the rich season of grandparenting, making the time for more love, care and fun, while passing on generational wisdom to the younger members of the family. Then there are those who have been called by God to foster and adopt, providing the gift of family while completely changing the trajectory of a child's life!

Yet, many have never experienced this expression of God's heart. Instead, their stories are marked by rejection, abandonment, conditional love, and even abuse. When we become a part of God's family, His desire is to "re-parent" us as our Heavenly Father. He can fill in the missing gaps of our lives by revealing to us His character and ways in the Scriptures and loving us through meaningful relationships that He blends into our lives to bring healing, hope, and life.

Rooted in God

- He is the "God of Abraham, the God of Isaac, and the God of Jacob" (Exodus 3:5–7). Notice the three generations of family life here: grandfather, father, and son!
- One of His favorite names to be identified as is Father (Isaiah 9:6; Matthew 6:9–14).
- He refers to us as sons and daughters, adopting us as His children (2 Corinthians 6:18; Galatians 4:4–7).
- He chose a people to be called and identified by His name (Deuteronomy 28:9–10).
- The Church, made up of God's people, is affectionately referred to as His Bride (Ephesians 5:25–33; Revelation 19:7, 21:9).

The Church

Although every follower of Jesus is a part of His Church, there are those called by God to lead various expressions of His Church. Many are local, although for some, their call is global (a focus of service that goes beyond a single location).

In reading the New Testament's Book of Acts, what we see emerge in and through the Church—while hitting bumps along the way—is a life-transforming and world-impacting power that advanced God's Kingdom throughout the known world of the time!

Their reference points for leading the Church came from walking with Jesus. Throughout the Book of Acts, we see them referencing these core four expressions of the Kingdom:

- *The Centrality of God's Presence*—From the beginning to the end of Acts, the centrality of God's presence—experiencing His nearness and encountering His transformational power—is evidenced in worship and prayer, the declaring of the Scriptures, sharing their faith, in signs and wonders, etc.
- *Walking in Community*—The Church in Acts loved and cared much for one another, walking in one heart and one mind. The way they gave sacrificially of their time and resources to meet one another's needs was winsome to the world around them!
- *Making Disciple Makers*—Being commissioned by Jesus to "teaching them to obey everything I have commanded you" (Matthew 28:18–20 NIV), His disciples poured all they could into new followers, to the point they could go and reproduce the same in others!
- *Local & Global Outreach*—Acts 1:8 guided their approach to outreach, meeting needs, and bringing God's love and

power to "Jerusalem (local) and in all Judea (regional) and Samaria (cross-cultural), and to the end of the earth (peoples and nations)."

<u>Rooted in God</u>

- Shepherd (Hebrews 13:10; 1 Peter 2:24–25, 5:4)
- Great High Priest (Hebrews 4:14–15)
- Immanuel, "God with us" (Matthew 1:22–23)
- Lord of the Harvest (Luke 10:1–2)
- Head of the Church (Ephesians 1:22–23, 4:15–16, 5:23)

Government, Law, and Nation Security

According to Romans 13:1–7, God ordains civil government, and its leaders have been given by God "for your good." This passage reminds us that all authority belongs to God. Since we live in a sin-filled, self-centered world, most people will not be ruled by the law of love—choosing one another's highest good—and therefore must be ruled by law.[1] "The design of civil government is to promote the security and the well-being of its citizens; and there would be no security of life and property, if there were no human governments."[2]

God has provided us with laws, such as the Ten Commandments, that reflect His character and ways and have everybody's best interest at heart. These laws, of course, apply to civil servants as well. Zacchaeus, a tax collector, repented when he became a Jesus-follower and made a four-fold restitution to all he had cheated (Luke 19:1–9). When civil laws are broken in society, it is the government's responsibility to punish the "wrongdoer" (Romans 13:3–4). It's interesting to note the principles behind the punishment meted out to the wrongdoer in the Old Testament: justice without partiality (Deuteronomy 13:6–10), without pity

(Deuteronomy 19:13–21), and without delay (Deuteronomy 25:1–3).

When it comes to nation security, roles such as police officers, firefighters, and soldiers are extensions of those in authority to secure and defend life, property, and the peace. Biblically, those serving in these roles are not to exercise unnecessary force, nor are they to extort those they are defending, or conquer for selfish gain (Luke 3:14).

Is society always ruled justly because a delegated-by-God government is in place? We know better than that by experience, don't we? Regardless, we need to live biblically: walking under authority (Romans 13:1–7), not speaking evil (Titus 3:1–2) and praying regularly for our leaders (1Timothy 2:1–4).

<u>Rooted in God</u>

- King of Kings and Lord of Lords (Revelation 17:14, 19:16)
- The Government will be upon His shoulder; Prince of Peace (Isaiah 9:6)
- The One who leads with Justice (Psalm 103:6–8; Isaiah 61:8; Revelation 15:1–4)
- The Lawgiver (Isaiah 33:21–22) and Righteous Judge (Psalm 96:11–13)
- Our Shield (Psalm 3:3), Protector (Psalm 68:4–6) and Deliverer (Psalm 18:1–3)

Education

A godly education begins in the home. God assigns parents the responsibility of training a child in His ways (Deuteronomy 6:6–8). Parents, then, involve others beyond the home who foster a child's heart and mind, natural abilities, and spiritual gifts, and add academic, physical, and other necessary skill sets. Together, this "team of guides"—drawn from local home-schooling networks, private or public schools—leads a child over the years to discovering their God-given calling/vocation.

To raise up a godly generation, educators must find ways to disciple kids. They can teach them to meet the needs of those around them, aid them in developing their character and gifts, help them cultivate healthy relationships, and encourage them to fulfill God's unique purposes for their lives. As they pass along knowledge and understanding, godly educators can also impart wisdom that comes from "the Fear of the Lord" (Proverbs 9:10). By relating well and modeling a godly life, a teacher can further God's Kingdom in a student's life.

Educators come in different shapes and sizes and serve in various capacities and roles. Some focus on pre-school children and others work with elementary students or middle-schoolers. There are those who teach high school, junior college, and university or graduate level students. Some are skilled to equip others in assorted trades. Administrators, principals, university professors, and presidents help make the educational process efficient and effective. Each one, doing what they do best, prepares students to engage the world around them.

Rooted in God

- The words "teach," "teaching," and "teacher" are mentioned in 266 verses in Scripture (ESV).
- God the Historian, making sure the events in Scripture were recorded for future generations.
- All knowledge, understanding, and wisdom are rooted in God (Colossians 2:1–3).
- We are to be deliberate about teaching the next generation (Psalm 78:1–8, 70–72).

- Part of the Great Co-Mission of Jesus is "teaching them to obey everything I have commanded you" (Matthew 28:18–20 NIV).

Media

Today's media shapes values, molds minds, and sways principles of people around the globe. It is powerful and persuasive. Its various vehicles offer tremendous services by affording us vital information, knowledge for decision-making, and awareness of what's happening. At its best, the media enables us to keep our lives well informed and our families safe. It also provides a necessary societal equilibrium, adding "checks and balances" to the potential abuses of power that can happen in government or in any other expression of leadership within society.

In today's world, sizeable media groups championing particular agendas feed the consumerism of our times and pad pockets for personal or political gain. Too often, "truth telling" is lost in the hours of endless analysis and personal opinions. Sometimes, the media lacks wisdom when being "the first" on a news story, reporting information falsely or incompletely. As a result, lives and reputations are left in ruins while the chase for the next story begins.

Disciples of Jesus need to participate in media of all kinds—electronic, print, digital, and social—for the sake His Kingdom. They need to disseminate information, communicate truth, and share fascinating stories to encourage others. Men and women who live their lives in great humility and the Fear of the Lord, and are willing to counter the pride, self-exaltation, and the fear of man that often dominates this vocational field, can be uniquely positioned to use their God-given skills to serve many.

Rooted in God

- Jesus is referred to in the Scriptures as the Word (John 1:1; Revelation 19:11–16).
- All truth is rooted in Him (John 8:30–32, 14:6).
- He is the Faithful Witness (Revelation 1:4–6, 3:13–15).
- Jesus was a storyteller (see His many parables in the Gospels).
- He is our banner (Exodus 17:14–16) and source (Hebrews 2:10–12, 5:8–10).

Arts, Entertainment, and Sports

In Exodus 35:31–34, we see an example of God pouring out His Spirit on those within this vocation,

...and he has filled him with the Spirit of God, with skill, with intelligence, with knowledge, and with all craftsmanship, to devise artistic designs, to work in gold and silver and bronze, in cutting stones for setting, and in carving wood, for work in every skilled craft.

A beautiful image emerges on a canvas. An actor, with sword in hand, fights with hundreds in the battle of his life on film. A dancer moves purposely with eye-pleasing ease and grace on a stage. At a ballpark, a bat hits a ball that soars through the night lights over a fence some 400 feet away. A sumptuous meal prepared on a plate with such imagination and artistry that it is only surpassed by its palate-pleasing deliciousness. A captivating chorus with words that we identify with invites us to join in at a concert (or through our earbuds!).

Arts, entertainment, and sports provide us with incredible and unique ways to see, taste, hear, smell, and touch life! They greatly impact us and "light us up" deep within, creating lifetime loves and loyalties to our favorite expressions. Without them, life would likely be more monotonous, causing us to miss out on incredible beauty, the richness of colors and sounds, the wealth of stories that need to be told, and the encountering kinds of experiences that add to the joy of sharing life with one another.

Creatives of all kinds, and athletes, are often given a unique and broad platform by which they can glorify God. Because of this, there is often much "heart work" needed to be done, so seeking out disciple makers who can help them cultivate humility, servanthood, generosity, and the habit of hearing and obeying God is essential.

Rooted in God

- God is the creator of heaven and Earth (Genesis 1–2).
- God expresses His joy through singing and dance (Zephaniah 3:17).
- The discipline of the Lord is like that of a coach training athletes for the prize (1 Corinthians 9:25–27).
- God made the first garments (Genesis 3:21), displays beauty through them (Exodus 28:1–3).
- The hospitality and culinary expression is rooted in God, as He was the first to provide a place to stay and food for Adam and Eve (Genesis 1–3).

Business and Commerce

Whether large sprawling corporations, regional franchises, small local businesses, or "mom and pop operations," every community is made up of these purveyors of products and services. Consider how many people businesses interact with on a regular basis, from customers and clients to vendors to other business leaders and community influencers. It's often the business leaders who rise up to address community concerns while also wielding influence in establishing public policy—locally, nationally, or globally. Of course, they also play a major role in society by generating and supplying wealth.

Although we sometimes like to think so, we really are not the "owners" of our businesses, but, rather, the stewards. As disciples of Jesus, we are to steward well what He places in our hands: abilities, skills and gifts, relationships and contacts, platforms of influence, products developed, and services created. When used under God's oversight and in obedience to Him, there is no limit to what He can do through business leaders. And when these leaders are willing to team together, they can bring the kind of positive change to their communities that makes a real difference in the lives of people.

One of the things I love about business leaders is that when they capture a vision, they're all over it—like bees on honey—to make it happen! They are not only good leaders, but good teammates you can count on. If you are called to this vocation, you are greatly needed to disciple the next generation, helping them to understand the world of business through the grid of Jesus' character, ways, and mission.

Rooted in God

- God owns it all (Deuteronomy 10:14; 1 Chronicles 29:11; Psalm 50:10–12; Haggai 2:8).
- He is the Landowner (Matthew 21:33–46); the Wise Builder (Matthew 7:24–27); the Vinedresser (John 15).
- He expects a return on His investment (Matthew 25:14–30).

- His central focus is the Kingdom, not money (Matthew 6:24, 33).
- He cares about those who work for Him (Ephesians 6:5–9).

Science and Technology

Since God is the author of both the Scriptures and science, there is complete harmony between them. As Galileo (1564–1642), wrote, "The world is the work and the Scriptures the word of the same God."[3] Johannes Kepler (1571–1630), a German mathematician and astronomer, and a contemporary of Galileo's, expressed it this way, "The tongue of God and the finger of God cannot clash."[4]

Kepler, whose discovery of the three laws of planetary motion laid the foundation for Sir Isaac Newton's theory of gravity, was a devout follower of Jesus. He regarded his study of the physical universe as "thinking God's thoughts after Him." He saw himself as "a high priest in the book of nature, religiously bound to alter not one jot or tittle of what it had pleased God to write down in it."[5]

Over the last century-plus, the gap between God and science has widened. There is a tremendous need for godly men and women who call science their vocation to step into this gap and shape hearts and minds with the wonder of God's Word and works.

Technology represents the most remarkable advancement in our lifetime. When I realize that I hold significantly more power and memory in the little iPhone in my hands than the astronauts had on board Apollo 11 when it went to the moon—it is staggering![6] The supersonic speed of change in this field, and the ability to serve and impact so many around the world for good, is equally astonishing. How does Jesus intend for us to use technology for

His Kingdom purposes? How do we make sure that technology is there to serve us and that we don't become enslaved to it?

<u>Rooted in God</u>

- God is the inventor of all creation, from molecules to man to Mars (Acts 3:15; Genesis 1–2).
- It's for Him, by Him, and through Him that all things exist (Romans 11:36; Hebrews 2:10).
- He's unsearchable (Psalm 145:3; Isaiah 40:28).
- When considering Internet speeds, we must reference how it pales to "God speed" and His instantaneous awareness, knowledge, and understanding of everything (Romans 11:33–34)!
- He's the source of wonder (Exodus 15:11; Job 5:8–9; Psalm 77:14).

Health, Medicine, and Wholeness

Those called to this vocation have the opportunity of coming alongside people in some of their greatest moments of need—not only with their expertise and skill, but also by tending and treating people as created in God's image with great value and for great purpose. Healthcare is an extension of God's heart for people— through wellness coaching and prevention, through medical and hospital care, or through wholeness of body, soul, and spirit. Those serving in this field recognize the interconnectedness of our beings and how one area may affect the others.

God has called doctors, nurses, dentists, and medical professionals of all kinds to serve people. They help us with our hearts, eyes, teeth, skin, feet, allergies, knees, backs, and everything else that can possibly act up in our bodies. They have a God-given ability to take the knowledge they've received and combine it with the skills they've been trained in to help physically heal and, at times, rescue lives. They, too, are an extension of God's heart and hands of healing. Many become specialists, providing us with the understanding and unique care we need to be made well.

Some called by Jesus to this vocation focus on wholeness of soul and spirit, and others on physical wellness. Counselors aim to aid people in getting well on the inside: emotionally, mentally or spiritually. They wisely guide people out of the "stuck places" of their lives and into ones marked by joy, peace, hope, and health! Others use their gifts and experience to focus on the physically fit side of wellness, through eating well, drinking plenty of water, exercising regularly, taking proper supplements, and getting enough rest.

Rooted in God

- God is our Maker (Psalm 95:6–7).
- He's our Source of Care (Psalm 27:10; 1 Peter 5:6–7) and the Giver of Life (Job 33:4).
- He's our Physician (Luke 8:43–48) and Healer (Exodus 15:26).
- Our Counselor (Isaiah 9:6), Consoler and Comforter (Psalm 23:4; 2 Corinthians 1:3–4).
- Our Trainer (1 Corinthians 9:24–25; 1 Timothy 4:8).

Environment, Agriculture, and Zoology

It all began in a garden created by God. He placed within it land, water, plants, trees, fish, birds, and animals of all kinds. When He created Adam and Eve, He placed them in that garden to work it and keep it as His stewards of His creation (Genesis 2:15).

Have you ever paused to consider that some of our current environmental issues may be rooted in sin, such as selfishness and greed? For example, consider water pollution. How hard is it to make sure we don't put something in our water, as a person or as a business, which causes it to be contaminated? When we pollute our waters, by acts of carelessness or for profitability, others "downstream"—whether literally or generationally—won't enjoy the same blessings from it as we do.

God, as the first Gardener, is concerned about fields, crops, land, and even how food we grow is shared with the hungry (Leviticus 25–26). Hunger and malnutrition are rampant throughout the world, as approximately one out of nine of us do not have enough food to lead a healthy, active life! Those in the vocation of farming can play a very significant role in making an impact here on behalf of Jesus and His Kingdom.

A reading of Psalm 104 reveals God's provision of food, water, and places to dwell for animals, these special creatures of His making. Whether furry friends that live with us in our homes, animals on the farm, or those in the wild, it's important to reference God's truths of humility, justice, and kindness as we interact with them.

Environment, agriculture, and zoology affect all of us around the world. We need those called to this vocational field to reference God's heart and wisdom, from the Scriptures, to create a godly path that serves both current and future generations well.

Rooted in God

- God is the creator of it all (Genesis 1:11–12, 1:20–21, 1:24–25).
- God relates to all His creation (Psalm 96:10–13; Isaiah 43:20–21; Job 37:14–18).
- His creation expresses worship to Him (Psalm 19:1; Isaiah 55:12–13; Revelation 5:13).

- He protects and preserves His creation (Genesis 6:19–21, 9:8–13).
- He uses nature to instruct us (Job 12:7–10; Proverbs 6:6–11; Romans 1:19–20).

Nonprofits and Service Organizations

Gathering boys and girls to participate in organized athletics. Distributing food and clothing to those in need. Taking care of families during health emergencies. Translating the Scriptures into a native tongue. Giving blood. Facilitating mentoring opportunities for those with limited adult leadership in their lives. Raising money for people with physical challenges. Providing resources for the arts. Protecting wildlife. Responding to those affected by natural disasters. Connecting needy children with sponsors. Developing societal leaders with godly character, wisdom, and perspective. Picking up roadside trash. Educating single moms to raise their children. Providing places for families to stay during a loved one's cancer treatment. Rescuing children and youth from the snares of human trafficking. Digging wells so entire villages have clean water to drink. This list of the impact made by nonprofits and service organizations could go on and on!

One of the things you'll notice about people who lead and serve in this vocation is their passion and commitment. They are cause-led and mission-dedicated. A need surfaces, an opportunity to make a real difference in people's lives emerges, a way to change the culture around them in a positive way arises—and not far behind is a man or woman with a vision of a better future. They engage this newfound opportunity with great desire and tireless commitment, rallying others, raising funds, and running volunteers through training so they can multiply their impact. They make a real difference in families, neighborhoods, their communities, and the world.

The ever-present needs for these groups, when it comes to fulfilling their missions, are volunteers (always needing more), organizational assistance (special skills like organization, technology, and communication) and, of course, funding for projects and annual expenses (donors, tithing companies, and foundations). How might you and your vocation come alongside a local nonprofit or service organization that your heart is linked to?

<u>Rooted in God</u>

- He is merciful and just (Psalm 69:16; 103:2–5,8; Deuteronomy 10:17–18).
- He gives hope to the hopeless (Psalm 62:5, 42:5).
- He is present for the poor and needy, the widow and orphan (Psalm 12:5; 34:6; Luke 4:18; Psalm 68:5; 146:9).
- He is a companion to the hungry, thirsty, stranger, naked, sick, and the prisoner (Matthew 25:31–46).
- He is a very present help, stronghold, and refuge in the day of trouble (Psalm 46:1–3; Nahum 1:7).

Peoples

Jesus loves people. He made them diverse and dispersed them around the globe. Groups of people naturally gravitate toward those with which they have in common, forming an identity and creating culture. Cultures represent such things as shared heritage, family systems, language, food, clothing, mutual interests and needs, and similar aims. These traits bind a group of people together and are reinforced by the way they relate to each other over time. Some people have Jesus' heart for certain groupings of people, and they are called by Him to lay down their lives in service for them.

Each grouping of people has been given a unique deposit from God that accentuates certain attributes of His character and conveys a distinctiveness of call. Have you ever considered that God has a call upon groups of people just like He does on individuals? Have you noticed that through various people, certain things are created, developed, and distributed to serve and bless other people?

Are you called by God to give yourself in the service of a certain people grouping? If so, consider what attributes of His character He desires to put on full display through them. What is their calling as a people? What are their redemptive gifts, and how has Satan tried to hinder them from fully expressing them?

What a glorious day it will be when we experience together the scenario foreshadowed in Revelation 5:9,

And they sang a new song, saying, "Worthy are you to take the scroll and to open its seals, for you were slain, and by your blood you ransomed people for God from every tribe and language and people and nation...

Rooted in God
- He's made people in His image representing every nation (Genesis 1:26–27; Psalm 86:9).
- He's the redeemer of nations (Revelation 5:9).
- He's the discipler of nations (Matthew 28:18–20).
- He's worshipped by kings and nations (Revelation 21:22–26).
- He's Messiah to the Jews and Savior to all people (Luke 1:30–33).

AIMING FOR APPLICATION

1. What vocational field(s) are you currently engaged in?

2. Beyond what is mentioned, where do see your vocation represented in the Scriptures?

3. What scriptural truths have you discovered that shape your vocational thinking or actions?

CHAPTER 5

Wisdom to Work With

S hortly after the 9/11 tragedy in our country, several of our pastors had a conversation about the need to expose our high schoolers to broader things beyond the "bubble" they tended to live life in. We desired for them to grow spiritually and be exposed to good leaders who had to think more broadly. This launched a plan to select and invite two dozen or so of our juniors and seniors into a year of being discipled spiritually and in leadership. As part of that year, each spring, we would take them for a week to Washington, D.C., to interact with relationships we had there that could broaden their horizons in many ways.

Around this same time, I had been invited to serve as a spiritual overseer for a church that was being planted in D.C. by some dear friends of mine. One of the young men that I was introduced to, who was part of the church, worked there in the heart of the government. During Brett's career, he had already had opportunities to serve in roles on the local, state, and national levels. I liked his heart after God and his genuine desire to grow as a disciple of Jesus. Brett had some great character qualities built within him, and I found that he was always very open and teachable. As we began to build a friendship, he invited me to speak into his life both personally and vocationally.

I launched our discipling relationship by introducing Brett to what the Scriptures say about the Fear of the Lord, a topic I believed would be very significant to his life, relationships, and vocation. I defined the Fear of the Lord for him as "reverencing and referencing God in all that you do." As he read a book that I gave him on the subject and processed it in conversation together, it was very apparent that this truth was making a deep impression upon his heart and mind. Shortly after, the Lord provided him with an opportunity to apply it to his vocation.

While serving as senior staff on a political campaign, where there is an amazing amount of pressure put on people to win an election, Brett encountered one of those "grey areas" that often exist in his vocation. He was approached about receiving a donation to the campaign that would have been very helpful in a tough election year. However, he felt there was something "off" about this particular donation. So, he ran it by their attorney, who told him that they would figure out a way to accept it—after all the end always justifies the means, including winning an important election!

Even though Brett got a green light from his attorney, he couldn't hurdle the huge red light flashing in his own heart. So, he sought the Lord in prayer, and pursued godly counsel. In the end, he yielded to that new sense of the Fear of the Lord within him and declined the donation. The truth of Proverbs 9:10, "The Fear of the Lord is the beginning of wisdom," had begun to take hold of his heart, providing him with godly wisdom to work with. In the years since then, I've watched Brett become a man who walks in the Fear of the Lord, serving as a godly reference point for his life, his family, and vocation!

*****

Before moving forward to connect calling and vocations with the Great Co-Mission and disciple making, I want to share some wisdom to work with that I have passed on over the years as godly reference points to those I've discipled who are serving throughout various vocational fields. These will help you represent God well within your vocation, benefit you in guarding your own heart and mind, and assist you in relating well with those you work with. They are also things you can begin to model with those you work with.

Measures of Capacity & Influence

I'm sure you've noticed in life and within your vocation that people seem to have various degrees of capacity, as well as influence. For example, one person may have the capacity to excellently reproduce the exact same product over and over again, while another person uses their creative and strategic thinking to constantly launch new products and services. One would rather work as part of a team and not have to supervise anybody, while another loves leading teams and overseeing many. Some like to come alongside to help leaders, while others like to develop leaders.

Ultimately, we need to come to a peaceful place of understanding and embrace our own measures of capacity and influence, knowing that God knows what He is doing—in and through our lives, and for His Kingdom!

There is a Greek word that appears thirteen times in eleven verses in the New Testament that can be a help to us here. It's the word *metron*. Among other places, it shows up in Romans 12 and Ephesians 4, where Paul is addressing the gifts and callings of Jesus followers. It means "a measuring rod" and is the root of such common words today as meter and speedometer. It speaks of a "determined extent, allotted measure, specific portion, limited degree."

In Romans 12:3 we find *metron* translated as "measure." The word is located right after the exhortation to be "transformed by the renewal of your mind" and right before the listing of various spiritual gifts. It says,

> *... by the grace given to me I say to everyone among you not to think of himself more highly than he ought to think, but to think with sober judgment, each according to the measure of faith that God has assigned.*

The word "assigned" in this verse means "to apportion, divide, impart, bestow, distribute a thing among a people."

The following verse, in Romans 12:4, states that although we are one body,

> *"...the members do not all have the same function."*

Verse 6 says,

"Having gifts that differ according to the grace given us, let us use them."

What is Paul saying in these passages? God is the one who "assigns, bestows and distributes" various "specific portions and allotted measures." Our gifts differ according to God's choosing and grace, and how we function within our gifts varies based on God's design.

God apportions measures of both capacity and influence on each one us. He gives a *measure of capacity*, which are God-given abilities, skills, and gifts that He puts in our lives to serve and bless others. He also gives each of us a *measure of influence*, which relates to whom and how many He graces us to serve, shape, oversee, and impact.

It's important that we recognize that God is our source of both capacity and influence, and He is the author of how they flow through our lives. As He combines our measures of capacity and influence with our various heritages, upbringings, personalities, experiences, and relationships, it allows us to uniquely co-mission with Him for Kingdom purposes.

Let me illustrate capacity and influence by looking briefly at ten people from throughout the Scriptures.

1. Abraham had a God-given capacity for stewarding property and wealth. His measure of influence was to be a blessing to all families of the earth.
2. Moses had the capacity to be a deliverer for Israel. His measure of influence was the children of Israel and the Pharaoh of Egypt.
3. Joshua had the capacity to be a conqueror of nations. The measure of influence for him was the tribes of Israel and the land of Canaan.

4. David had been given the capacity by God to be king. His first measure of influence was over his sheep, then after proving faithful there, God made him king of Israel.

5. Esther had the capacity to serve as a nation's queen. Her measure of influence was the king, on behalf of the people of Israel.

6. Jonah had a capacity to bring the Word of the Lord. His place of influence was the city of Nineveh.

7. Mary had the capacity by the Holy Spirit to be the mother of the Son of God. Her measure of influence was Jesus and her other children.

8. Paul had an apostolic pioneering capacity and his measure of influence was Gentiles, kings, and the children of Israel.

9. Priscilla had a capacity to teach, and her measure of influence was her husband, Aquila, the church in their home, Apollos, and the Apostle Paul.

10. Lydia had the capacity to be a businesswoman, and her measure of influence included the city of Thyatira.

Note that each one had a specific *measure of capacity*— abilities, skills, and gifts given by God. Each also had a *measure of influence*, determined by God. Once you understand the measures of capacity and influence assigned to you, it helps you work within the context of what Jesus wants to do through you. It also keeps you from drifting outside the areas where God has graced you to serve, or from being caught in the comparing-out-of-insecurity trap.

I have two very dear pastor friends, each functioning well in their gifts. One is a gifted teacher and the other is an effective organizational leader—these represent their measures of capacity. God has assigned one to serve a large flock that is making an impact both nationally and internationally, and the other leads a medium-sized congregation that is making a huge mark in their local community—these are their measures of influence. Both are God-given. Both are obeying Jesus. Both are wonderfully advancing God's Kingdom within their assigned measures of capacity and influence.

Joshua didn't try to be like Moses, looking for another people in bondage to deliver. Instead, he functioned within his God-ordained capacities and influence and helped Israel secure the Promised Land. Paul, tired from a missionary journey, didn't just decide to stay in Ephesus and pastor. Instead, he fulfilled his apostolic capacity and influence by furthering the message of Jesus among those who had not yet heard it. The New Testament letters that he wrote, Romans through Philemon, continue to influence generations of Jesus followers. That, too, is part of Paul's extended God-given influence!

Work is Worship

While serving as a missionary in YWAM, we would hold several all-hands-on-deck Saturday morning workdays each year. It was a time to deep clean, paint rooms and buildings, tackle big lawn care projects, and address any major facility maintenance concerns.

During my time there in Kona, we often had a guest from Indiana Wesleyan University speak at our base, Dr. Glenn Martin.[1] He was a tremendous teacher who shaped our thinking on living with a biblical worldview. One of the things he taught us that stuck was "work is worship." Shortly thereafter, our Saturday workdays became known as "Worship Days"!

Two things I want to highlight here. First, God is the one who initiated work. He works. He created the universe (Genesis 1 and 2) and He continues to advance His Kingdom. God's work is an overflow of who He is and what He does. Some view work as a consequence of sin, believing that if it wasn't for Adam and Eve's choices, we'd still be relaxing in a beautiful garden eating fruit to our heart's content! Not so. God assigned Adam and Eve to work and tend the garden well before (Genesis 2:5–16) the fruit was plucked from the tree and sin entered the world.

Second, all our work is to be done unto the Lord. Regardless of who is watching, we are ultimately working for His pleasure and glory. We should offer our full effort to whatever we have in front of us to do:

> *Whatever you do, work heartily, as for the Lord and not for men, knowing that from the Lord you will receive the inheritance as your reward. You are serving the Lord Christ.* (Colossians 3:23–24)

Every expression of work that we do—dishes after dinner, merging two companies, calling plays in the huddle on a football field, designing a new home or website, baking a pie for the widow next door, tending a contusion on a horse's hind quarters—can be done as worship "unto the Lord," and for His glory.

> *So, whether you eat or drink, or whatever you do, do all to the glory of God.* (1 Corinthians 10:31)

Kingdom Ambassadorship

A few years ago, I had the privilege of addressing ambassadors representing various nations around the world. These men and women were extremely gracious and diplomatic, and weighed what they said and did very carefully. You could see that although they were being themselves, they also knew they were not there to represent themselves. Rather, they recognized that their every expression was a reflection and representation of the leader and nation that had sent them.

Every follower of Jesus is an ambassador of God's Kingdom wherever they go and whomever they're with. At all times and in all places, you and I represent His character, ways, and mission. Paul's words to the believers in Colossae underscore this truth:

Whatever you do, in word or deed, do everything in the name of the Lord Jesus. (Colossians 3:17)

Os Guinness writes, "Calling means that our lives are so lived as a summons of Christ that the expression of our personalities and the exercise of our spiritual gifts and natural talents are given direction and power precisely because they are not done for themselves, our families, our businesses or even humankind, but for the Lord, who will hold us accountable for them."[2]

Over the last decade-and-a-half, I've walked alongside a Grammy Award-winning artist as a friend and disciple maker. Early in her career, though loving Jesus with all her heart, she had not fully made the connection between her calling and Kingdom ambassadorship. While chatting one day on the phone, an opportunity arose for me to share more with her about this. We talked about how those within her vocation tend to look for a "stage" to perform on so people can see and hear them. We then spoke about her calling, as a follower of Jesus, and how she didn't need a "stage," but instead, has been given a "platform" by God to represent Him through her very public vocation. That was a game-changing moment in her life, and now as a disciple maker herself, she passes this same truth on to the young artists she's investing the things of God within!

You have been sent by Jesus to represent Him in your vocational field within society. Being His ambassador is your primary reason for being there! Now, you might not be in your ultimate role just yet, but He is using this time to shape and add to you, to teach you His ways, and to touch the lives of those around you. Who knows? Maybe as you're reading this, you are realizing that you are not really where you are supposed to be right now. That's okay. Jesus is always glad to reposition you where He wants you, as you humble yourself, seek Him in prayer, and glean from the godly counsel of those He has brought around you.

Conscious of Your Conscience

Tentmaker, disciple-maker, and writer of thirteen of our New Testament books, the Apostle Paul said,

> *So I always take pains to have a clear conscience toward both God and man.* (Acts 24:16)

Our vocational calling is not ultimately to something but to someone—the Lord Jesus. We adopt His character, ways, and mission, as revealed in the Scriptures, as our sole standard and uncompromising point of reference. As His disciples, we want to do nothing that ever diminishes His character in someone's eyes, taints the goodness of His ways, or misrepresents His mission to a watching world. Like Paul, we must "take pains" to make sure we are walking cleanly in our conscience with God and the people around us.

Our conscience functions like an inner truth rudder. It is sharpened by the Word of God and calibrated by the Holy Spirit living within us. When we detach from what the Scriptures teach and become unresponsive to the nudges of the Holy Spirit, we find ourselves drifting into the waters of compromise. It happens subtly, one small turning from the truth at a time. Done often enough, we become disoriented and become more vulnerable to deception. If we continue this trajectory, we become acclimated to, and even defend, a virtual reality that is far from the course of where we once sailed with a clear conscience before God and man.

Luther worked as a campus pastor, college professor, biblical scholar, and writer. He understood that while functioning within his vocation, he needed to be true to the Scriptures and his conscience. When asked to recant his writings to the pope before Emperor Charles V at the Diet of Worms, Luther references his conscience in defending himself. When asked, "Will you recant?" he simply replies, "I am bound by the Scriptures I have quoted and my conscience is captive to the Word of God. I cannot and I will not retract anything, since it is neither safe nor right to go against conscience. I cannot do otherwise, here I stand, may God help me. Amen."[3]

Luther's vocation was regulated by the Scriptures and his conscience. Bound by the truth of Scripture, it would not allow him to go against being faithful to God and his conscience, even if it meant losing his life. This is walking in the Fear of the Lord.

I have a leader friend who called me one day to tell me that Jesus had revealed to his heart that there was some restitution he had to make with a former boss. Before coming to know Jesus, he had taken some items related to his job that he now realized were not his. Because he desired to obey what the Lord had shown him and wanted to make right where he had been wrong, he reached out to his boss, humbled himself, and made things right.

That's being conscious of your conscience!

How have you handled your conscience regarding your vocation? Has it been clouded in the pursuit of status and position, the allure of sin, the buzz of celebrity, the chase of gain, or the sizzle of success? Have you walked in the Fear of the Lord or ignored the conviction of God within? If the latter, you can restore your inner truth rudder by responding in repentance toward God and making restitution toward people. Now would be a great time to move toward a clear conscience.

Ready to Reproduce

One more thought.

Have you ever paused to consider how the things of God that you've learned from the Scriptures, gleaned along the way from others, and embraced through experience, can be planted and grown in the lives of others? Whether it's how to forgive those who've brought hurt, or how to hear God in life decisions that must be made, or how to reflect godly character despite a bad boss or a messy situation at work. How does this stuff get embedded in the lives of others so they can live it, reflect it, and reproduce it?

Let me have the privilege of providing this answer for you.

It's through YOU!

That's right, YOU—YOU are Jesus' answer to how things get purposely passed on!

When Jesus was at the very end of His journey here on Earth, He spoke to His disciples in Matthew 28:18–20 and said,

> *And Jesus came and said to them, "All authority in heaven and on earth has been given to me.* **Go therefore and make disciples of all nations***, baptizing them in the name of the Father and of the Son and of the Holy Spirit,* **teaching them to observe all that I have commanded you***. And behold, I am with you always, to the end of the age.*

Disciples of Jesus are to reproduce more disciples for Jesus. They purposely pass on to others what Jesus has passed on to them.

That's called disciple making. It's what Jesus did, and it's what He's co-missioned us to do. It's His primary way of advancing His Kingdom on Earth. As we shape those God brings our way in His character, ways, and mission, they reflect Him in their lives, relationships, and vocations!

Several years ago, while participating in the National Prayer Breakfast in Washington, D.C., I had the wonderful opportunity of meeting with some godly young leaders. As is often the case in our nation's capital, these were sharp men and women in their late-twenties to mid-thirties who were going places in their fields. As we talked together about life and leadership, the topic of disciple making emerged. During our conversation, one of the women spoke up, and with some measured frustration said to me, "Dave, we can't find anyone willing to give us their time to pour into us. We've looked. We know we need it. How do we find disciple makers for our lives?"

Although not surprised, my heart was deeply saddened when I heard this. I responded with what first came to my heart, asking them to forgive me and those older than them, for missing out on the privilege of discipling them in the things of God. I reminded them of how valuable they are in the eyes of Jesus and how they, as a generation, are so worth investing time, effort, resources, and the very best God has taught us into their lives and leadership.

Who around you—in your relationships and vocation—has this same need for somebody to shape them in God's ways? Many more than you can even imagine, desperately need it, want it, and are waiting for someone to step up to do it.

What about you? Have you been discipled? Are you ready to reproduce disciple makers?

If you're like about 80% of other followers of Jesus in our world today, your response may be, "No, I don't think so."

No worries! In our next few chapters, you'll begin to learn all about The Great Co-Mission of disciple making: Jesus' vision for it and how He did it, how you can participate in it, its role related to your vocation, identifying who you can be pouring into—and much more!

AIMING FOR APPLICATION

1. What is your current measure of capacity and influence?

2. Which one of these wisdom pieces spoke most loudly to you? What will you do with it?

3. Which ones are you currently living out, giving you authority to disciple others in?

CHAPTER 6

The Disciple Maker's Aim & Ingredients

L iving in Nashville means you are surrounded by singers, songwriters, musicians, sound and lighting technicians, etc. Some have just moved to town and are hoping for their big break, while others are well established, some are known throughout the world, others within the industry, and some have earned their highest respect right here in town. Because many of them are often on the road with their bands, we find other ways to walk alongside and disciple them and their families.

One day, I received a call from Eva, an emerging artist I had recently met and began to disciple. I had found her to be sincere, a growing follower of Jesus, and someone who was open to others speaking into her life. While on this call, Eva asked if I'd pray for her and her family as they embarked on a country-wide radio tour, a journey that would bring exposure to her and her music via radio stations playing her songs and interviewing her. I told her I'd be glad to, so we prayed together on the phone.

As we were praying, I felt the Lord put an impression within my heart specifically for Eva. I asked if I could share something that the Lord had put on my heart for her, and she graciously welcomed it. This was an opportunity to disciple her further around God's ways. I shared with her how, regardless of a person's status in life or celebrity, Jesus always calls us as His disciples to look for ways to serve those around us, to better and bless their lives. As Eva listened, she was tracking with me and wholeheartedly agreed! So, we talked together about what this may look like and we came up with a plan that would allow her to practice servanthood while on her radio tour.

Upon arriving at her radio tour stops, Eva would kindly acknowledge autograph seekers with her eyes (knowing she could come back soon and sign for them), while she first sought out the station manager or person who had invited her to come. She would approach them, introduce herself and her family (not assuming they knew "who she was"), then she would ask them how they, as a family, could serve them as a radio station while they were with them that day. Eva was excited to give this a try and committed to do so!

After nearly two months of being on the road, we grabbed a meal with Eva and her family at a local Cracker Barrel to catch up. I was very curious to hear how her "servanthood experiment" had gone. She told me what God had done, and that He had used her serving others as a game-changer in her own life! As her career soon took off, this expression of the ways of God had taken hold of Eva. It remains a vital part of how she views those she works with and the audiences she performs before.

In a vocation where self-absorption can often take center stage, I know that Eva, who since has received the highest annual performance award in her musical genre, makes her aim not only to be successful in singing, but also in serving God and others above herself! Disciple making makes a difference in a person's life and practically touches those they serve via their vocation!

*****

One of the statistics that spoke most loudly to me from the Barna Group's research on work and vocation, among those who actively try to integrate their faith and work, was the fact that when asked what a Christian's responsibility was in the workplace, the deliberate expression of disciple making did not even make the list!

1. Act ethically–88%
2. Speak the truth–88%
3. Demonstrate morality–87%
4. Do excellent work to glorify God–83%
5. Practice humility–81%
6. Serve others–79%
7. Make friends with non-Christians–78%
8. Help bring grace and peace to others–75%
9. Speak out against unfairness or injustice–75% vs all Christian workers: only 53%
10. Withstand temptation–79%
11. Help mold the culture of my workplace–72%
12. Share the Gospel–44%[1]

Over the years, I have discovered that many sincere followers of Jesus do not understand what disciple making is or how to go about it, in their relationships or vocations. Because most have never been deliberately discipled by another further-along follower of Jesus, they don't have a grid of how important the role of disciple making is to play in their lives. In the next few chapters, we'll take a closer look at it, including diving deeper into key pieces of disciple making: the aim; the ingredients; the process of transformation; and the tools.

The Aim

Jesus had a blueprint—a model, a pattern, a prototype—for spiritually developing His twelve disciples! These men who followed Jesus were not just "buddies" who tagged along so He had some company through life's journey. Rather, they were called and purposely prepared by Jesus to carry on His Kingdom work to impact generations to come! They were discipled by Jesus so that His character, ways, and mission would be reflected and reproduced through their lives!

Let's begin by defining what we mean by disciple making.

Just so we are clear, leading someone to Jesus is simply the first step toward becoming a disciple. It is the beginning, not the end. Unfortunately, we often have a church culture that views "getting saved" as the end game. After all, their sins are forgiven, and they are going to heaven! However, as much as we rejoice in that reality, we need to also be ready to reproduce the life of Jesus within them!

Do you have a deliberate game plan of how to grow someone spiritually so that they reflect Jesus and can reproduce the same in others?

Do you know what to aim for?

I'd like to share with you the definition I have used as a reference point over the decades I've been practicing disciple making, which has built within it, our aim.

Reproducing the character, ways, and mission of Jesus in those around you, expecting them to multiply the same in others.

Read it again.

One more time, please.

This is what disciple making looked like for Jesus! This was His aim. He reproduced within His disciples His character, His ways, and His mission, then later expected them to reproduce the very same in those around them. *First, it was to be reflected in them; then, reproduced through them.*

Let's break down the "reproducing the character, ways, and mission of Jesus" part a bit.

The Character of Jesus

From the moment we respond to Jesus, the Holy Spirit begins conforming us into His likeness—shaping us to reflect His character (Romans 8:29) through our personalities and gifts. From Genesis to Revelation, the character of God is put on display! He continuously reveals Himself to His people through His names, titles, and attributes in Scripture, providing us with remarkable portraits of who He really is. We may not see Him with our eyes, but He is in plain view throughout the Scriptures. His character reveals who He really is! It is so awesome that Revelation 4:8 declares that the angels in heaven are endlessly responding to who He is by declaring,

Holy, Holy, Holy is the Lord God Almighty, who was and is and is to come!

When Philip asked to see the Father, Jesus replied, "Whoever has seen Me has seen the Father" (John 14:8–9). As we behold the life of Jesus, we can see what God is really like!

- How does Jesus show His heart to the weary?
  - He's the One who can give them rest, revealing God's heart of love and care.

- How does Jesus act towards the woman caught in adultery?
  - He reveals the Father's heart of mercy, forgiveness, and holiness.

- How does Jesus respond to the people He's around?
  - He reveals Himself as the Good Shepherd who cares for the sheep.

- How does Jesus relate to the sick and oppressed?
  - He heals them and sets them free, revealing Himself as Deliverer.

- How does Jesus act towards the Pharisees caught in their religiosity?
  - He challenges them, revealing Himself as the Truth.

- How does Jesus restore Peter after his denial?
  - By meeting him on his "turf" on the seashore, revealing Himself as Redeemer, Restorer.

The expressions of His character go on and on: justice, kindness, goodness, faithfulness, grace, truth, and compassion, to mention a few. His names call out His character as well: Abba Father, Advocate, I AM, Almighty God, Ancient of Days, Alpha & Omega, and Author of Life. And, these are just a few tied to the first letter of the alphabet!

When reproducing the character of Jesus in others, here are a couple of things you can do to help them.

First, have them read through the Scriptures focusing on God's character. Doing so can be a real life-changer! I referenced earlier that I decided to do this very thing, marking with purple pencil every name, title, and attribute of God's character that I ran across. It was remarkable how many different aspects of God's character I now saw—some I had seen before, but now I was seeing with a different lens; and then there were even more that I had never noticed at all! Now, whenever I open my Bible, I love that His character—highlighted in purple pencil—draws me in and invites me to know Him more!

Have you ever heard the saying, "You become what you behold?" The more we can point those we are discipling to behold who He really is in the Scriptures, the more He transforms them into His image.

Another way I like to help someone reflect God's character in their lives is by showing them how to pay attention when God is up to something within them. I often use the expression with those I'm pouring into, "your reactions are windows to your heart." Ever thought about that? What is going on deep inside of you—no matter how hard you are trying to mask it—is the "real you." And, the "real you" comes out in your reactions!

God is after the genuine transformation of your heart, replacing yours and giving you His, allowing His character to be revealed in and through your life.

> *And I will give you a new heart, and a new spirit I will put within you. And I will remove the heart of stone from your flesh and give you a heart of flesh. And I will put my Spirit within you, and cause you to walk in my statutes and be careful to obey my rules.* (Ezekiel 36:26–27)

How does God do this work within our hearts?

God begins by exposing the issues of our heart, things like sin, selfishness, and stuck places. He'll use the relational storms we are having with people, difficult situations we are facing in life, and those unbelievably challenging life circumstances before us to reveal what is really tucked down deep inside of our hearts. It reveals what we truly believe about God's character! As we see what's there, and in humility of heart embrace it through expressions like repentance and forgiveness, we journey toward becoming more like Jesus.

When discipling someone through this, lovingly point them to the Scriptures and what God reveals about Himself. Also, demonstrate God's character through your life as you walk alongside of them in this process of character transformation.

The Ways of Jesus

If God's character reveals "who" He is, His ways reveal "how" He does things! His ways are revealed all throughout the Scriptures. They are always wise, apply to people everywhere, and they work!

The Scriptures tell us in Isaiah,

For my thoughts are not your thoughts, neither are your ways my ways, declares the Lord. For as the heavens are higher than the earth, so are my ways higher than your ways and my thoughts than your thoughts. (Isaiah 55:8–9)

In Psalms, David said:

Make me to know your ways, O Lord; teach me your paths. (Psalm 25:4)

Moses cried out to God to show him His ways (Exodus 33:13–14) and we learn later in Psalms that He did exactly that:

He made known his ways to Moses, His acts to the people of Israel. (Psalm 103:7)

Jesus even referred to Himself as,

...the way... (John 14:6)

The ways of God reveal how He does things. For example:
- How to maintain a healthy marriage
- How to start a business or plant a church
- How to effectively lead people, both on task and in relationship
- How to discover and develop your life's purpose
- How to deal wisely in financial matters
- How to get free from the stuck places of your soul
- How to heal messed up relationships
- How to deal with employees
- How to raise your children

And on and on it goes throughout the Scriptures! Here are a few examples in the life of Jesus and how His ways might apply to our lives:

- As a disciple of Jesus, how do you go about making an important decision?
  - □ Jesus: When it came time to choose His disciples, Jesus spent an entire night seeking His Father's will in prayer (Luke 6:12–16).
  - □ In Your Life: Waiting on God in the place of prayer— seeking His heart and agenda—versus making your own decision and asking Him to bless it.

- As a disciple of Jesus, how am I to relate to others around me?
  - □ Jesus: He viewed and treated people with genuine love and great value, so much so that He died for them.
  - □ In Your Life: Romans 12:10 says, *Love one another with brotherly affection. Outdo one another in showing honor.* We are to walk with people—family, friends, neighbors, employees, etc.—based on love and honoring them above ourselves.

- As a disciple of Jesus, what's at the core of leadership?
  - □ Jesus: He taught that in the world around us, people try to "lord" things over others, jockeying for positions of importance. He modeled for His disciples how to lead through serving.
  - □ In Your Life: Those who are greatest in the Kingdom are those who serve others the most (Matthew 20:25–27). And, serving is not a ladder to leadership, rather serving is what leadership is all about!

As we make disciples, we must guide them into following God's ways, rooted in the Scriptures. Due to our upbringings, backgrounds, experiences, and life choices, we often find ourselves "stuck" in our own ways, following the course of this world (Ephesians 2:1–3). In becoming a disciple of Jesus, our minds begin to be renewed by the Holy Spirit from the inside out (Romans 12:1–2), as we "put off" the old self and "put on" the new (Ephesians 4:17–32). God's ways take hold in our lives as we look to obey the Scriptures and respond to what the Holy Spirit is doing in our lives.

We must disciple new disciples to understand that Jesus doesn't save us and then leave us struggling to do our very best to follow "His rules." Instead, the Holy Spirit comes and makes us His residence (1 Corinthians 6:19–20; Ephesians 5:18). In the process, He forms the ways of Jesus in us, so they overflow through us to touch the world.

The Mission of Jesus

As disciple makers, along with teaming with the Holy Spirit to form in disciples the character and ways of God, we must also develop within them a heart to participate in His mission. I view the mission of Jesus as the four wheels of a vehicle. Each of these four missional expressions are connected to the others, and they all have the same aim: to get us to join Jesus in what He's doing so He is glorified through our lives.

1. Jesus revealed what God is really like

The life of Jesus reveals what God is really like. Jesus said, *Whoever has seen me has seen the Father* (John 14:9). Jesus "fleshed out" God for us to see and experience Him more personally.

The image of God that we carry around in our hearts and minds affects the way we live our daily lives. When His image has been tainted in people's minds, through their own sin or being sinned against, the devil attempts to distort and disfigure God's character in their hearts and minds. Part of Jesus' mission through us is to provide people with a fresh and scripturally accurate picture of what He's really like. What He looks like with "skin on." That mission requires that we disciple those Jesus brings us in His character and ways. When people see Him for who He really is, they can't help but love Him and give their lives to Him!

2. Jesus reconciled people to God

Another "wheel" in the mission of Jesus is reconciling people to God. Sin has separated us all from Him, and His death on the cross and resurrection enables that relationship to be restored. Jesus said, referring to Himself in Luke 19:10,

For the Son of Man came to seek and to save the lost.

Throughout the Gospels, Jesus builds genuine relationships with people and meets their real needs. As a matter of fact, He spent so much time with needy people that others labeled Him the "friend of sinners" (Matthew 9:9–13, 11:19).

We've all been given the ministry of reconciliation.

All this is from God, who through Christ reconciled us to himself and gave us the ministry of reconciliation; that is, in Christ God was reconciling the world to himself, not counting their trespasses against them, and entrusting to us the message of reconciliation. Therefore, we are ambassadors for Christ, God making his appeal through us. (2 Corinthians 5:18–20)

By the way we live and relate, we should cause people to be drawn to the One we love who has changed our lives.

3. Jesus demonstrated God's Kingdom on Earth

The Lord's prayer (Matthew 6:9–11) includes, *Your kingdom come, your will be done on Earth as it is in heaven.* Jesus proclaimed the Kingdom of God throughout His entire ministry here on Earth. The Sermon on the Mount, in Matthew 5–7, is the centerpiece of Jesus' teaching on the Kingdom, while Matthew 13 contains numerous Kingdom parables that provide further insights into it.

The Kingdom finds expression wherever He is given Lordship. It advances as through us, He brings good news to the poor, binds up the brokenhearted, sets captives free, and replaces mourning with gladness (Isaiah 61:1–3). It advances as He destroys the works of the devil (1 John 3:8) so people can live their lives to the fullest (John 10:10). It's expressed as Jesus goes about doing good (Acts 10:38). His Kingdom is an everlasting Kingdom that will have no end (Psalm 145:13). And, Jesus teaches us to seek it first (Matthew 6:33)!

All of us have key roles to play within the Kingdom, using our gifts and vocations where He's appointed us to serve.

4. Jesus reproduced disciple makers

Let's remember that Jesus taught the crowds but was dedicated to investing in the Twelve. Imagine what you would do if you knew you had three years to deposit everything you could in a few people who would then launch the greatest movement in the history of the world! You would be very selective with whom you spent your time and deliberate about what you would pass on. Your priorities would be crystal clear and your focus firmly fixed.

Disciple making is the primary way through which Jesus reproduced His character, ways, and mission in others. If there was a better way, He would have done it. If a different way would have been more effective, He would have used it. It is the co-mission that He has invited me and you to join Him in to change the world!

So, reflecting the character, ways, and mission of Jesus in one's life, and then reproducing it in the lives of others, was the aim of Jesus. Is it mine? Is it yours?

Expecting Them to Multiply

Let's wrap this up by briefly looking at the latter part of our disciple making definition, "...expecting them to multiply the same in others."

In 2 Timothy 2:1–2, Paul, writing to Timothy states,

> *You then, my child, be strengthened by the grace that is in Christ Jesus, and what you have heard from me in the presence of many witnesses entrust to faithful men, who will be able to teach others also.*

Pictured here in this passage, is disciple making that goes four generations deep: (1) Paul discipled (2) Timothy, who discipled those who were (3) faithful, and those faithful ones discipled (4) others.

Discipling four generations deep needs to become the multiplying vision of every disciple of Jesus! Part of our aim must be making sure that those we've discipled know how to do the same with others! Without it, generational multiplication ceases. That is what has happened in our day. It's up to me and you to obey Jesus to see this making disciple makers jump-started once again.

In our next chapter, we'll get hands-on regarding how we can get started in making disciple makers!

The Ingredients

While working my way through the New Testament's book of Matthew, I observed four key ingredients of the disciple making blueprint of Jesus. Interestingly, I found these very same ingredients evident when His disciples reproduced His life in a second generation of disciples in the Book of Acts (more on that in the next chapter!). As you will notice, the Holy Spirit is right in the center of it all as the transformer. It is His lead we must follow as disciple makers.

In brief, here's what it looks like:

- As they walk alongside Him, the *teaching* of Jesus grows His disciples around His character, ways, and mission (e.g., the Sermon on the Mount in Matthew 5–7).
- Jesus invites them to walk alongside Him into relationship and in the context of *community* (beginning in Matthew 4:18–22).
- As He relates with and teaches them, He looks for them to be responsive to Him by *obeying* what He asks them to do (e.g., being sent out in Matthew 10, feeding the 5,000, Peter's walk on the water in Matthew 14).
- And, in the end, after His death and resurrection, He commissions them to *reproduce* in others what He had poured into them (Matthew 28:18–20).

Although His disciples surely didn't understand it at the time, Jesus was fully aware that He was laying the groundwork, through His disciples, for the largest and most powerful movement the world will ever know—His Kingdom expressed through His Church!

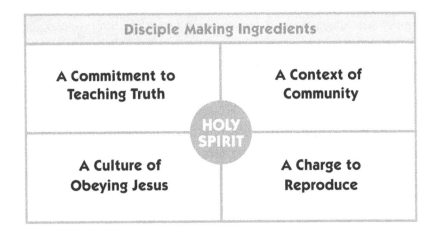

Let's take a little closer look at each of these ingredients.

The Holy Spirit

Our most important role in the disciple making process is to watch where the Holy Spirit seems to be working in someone's life and come alongside what He's doing. Of utmost importance is that we pay attention to what the Holy Spirit is revealing in those we are discipling. Then it's our responsibility to pray and come alongside them to encourage and help them obey what's been revealed. The reality is, we have the privilege of teaming with the Holy Spirit, following His lead in the disciple making journey!

A Commitment to Teaching Truth

Jesus was referred to as "Rabbi" or "Teacher" by the disciples. He was the source of their truth during their three years together. What He taught, why He taught what He did, and how He passed it on so that they owned it and could reproduce it is of great significance. Jesus made sure they really caught what He was teaching as He expected them to later do the same for others.

Jesus transformed the disciples' lives with the truths of His Kingdom. He often used the method of *teach—demonstrate— replicate* (more in a later chapter). He taught to the point of understanding, while demonstrating what it practically looked like, and then He asked His disciples to replicate it in front of Him.

We see an example of this in Matthew 14 in the story of the feeding of the 5,000. When the disciples see the massive amount of people present as the mealtime approached, they ask Jesus to send everyone away to nearby villages to buy food. However, Jesus responds with *They need not go away; you give them something to eat.* They'd heard Him teaching about faith numerous times, and now it seems He wants to stretch theirs by demonstrating His. They collect five loaves and two fish. Jesus blesses the meal and multiplies it to feed everyone present. And just to make the point sharper, there are twelve baskets left over, one for each of them!

In the very next scene, in the same chapter, Jesus, the "Teacher," moves them from demonstration to replication. While on a boat during a storm, Jesus comes walking to the disciples on the water! He invites Peter to join Him on the water, and Peter does! Peter replicates the faith Jesus had taught and what he had just seen demonstrated. Yes, fear ends up getting the best of Peter, but his faith got exercised and he walked on water!

A Context of Community

Jesus' disciple-making takes place in the context of relationships. He prayerfully hand-selected a small group of people to "be with Him" (Mark 3:14). Over a span of three years, this team rubbed shoulders and experienced the ups-and-downs and in-and-outs of relationships and life together!

Think about a group of people you've spent three years or more of your life with. It could be in college, in the military, on the job, as neighbors, as a ball team or band, or in a small group. Not only does an experience like this meld you together, but your lives also rub off on each other! You come to a place of valuing this environment where you are cared for, cheered on, and challenged.

This little band of men that Jesus brought together—including fishermen, a tax collector, a nationalist zealot—made up a unique community. Although they had similar upbringings, they had different passions, skill sets, interests, and life experiences that they brought to the table. No doubt Jesus knew walking together would expose their hearts, creating opportunities for Him to shape them more around His character and in His ways.

Through community, Jesus demonstrated for His disciples what love looks like, what it means for someone to lay down their life for another, what it's like to know someone will be with you always, through thick and thin. Jesus demonstrated the importance of interdependence, as well as forgiveness. Regardless of one's heritage or gender, the way He related to people made a mark on the Twelve. Walking alongside Jesus day-in-and-day-out modeled a vastly different way of viewing and living life than they had been previously accustomed to.

Relationships, and the context of community, was core to Jesus' expression of making disciples!

A Culture of Obeying Jesus

The life of Jesus was marked by obedience to His Father. He consistently did what He saw His Father doing.

> Jesus said to them, "Truly, truly, I say to you, the Son can do nothing of his own accord, but only what he sees the Father doing. For whatever the Father does, that the Son does likewise." (John 5:19)

This kind of obedience is not a "religious proving" or spiritual obligation, but rather an expression of deep love and affection for His Father. Born out of genuine relationship, this is a "get to" kind of obeying, not a "got to"!

Amongst His disciple making community, Jesus cultivated a culture—a way of life—of obeying Him. We are not talking here about a "blind obedience," but rather obedience based on knowing and walking with Jesus and experiencing firsthand for themselves His character and ways. Because of proven love and trust, they obey Jesus, knowing that He always had their highest good, and that of His Kingdom, in mind.

Jesus taught His disciples that obeying makes the difference between simply hearing the truth and being transformed.

Everyone then who hears these words of mine and does them will be like a wise man who built his house on the rock. And the rain fell, and the floods came, and the winds blew and beat on that house, but it did not fall, because it had been founded on the rock. And everyone who hears these words of mine and does not do them will be like a foolish man who built his house on the sand. And the rain fell, and the floods came, and the winds blew and beat against that house, and it fell, and great was the fall of it. (Matthew 7:24–27)

I like to say that "obedience is the engine of transformation"! In looking at the lives of Jesus' disciples, their "hearing and doing" led to transformed lives and the transforming of other's lives through theirs!

A Charge to Reproduce

After three years of walking with Jesus in community, being taught His ways, and developing habits of obedience, He then says,

All authority in heaven and on earth has been given to me. Go therefore and make disciples of all nations, baptizing them in the name of the Father and of the Son and of the Holy Spirit, teaching them to observe all that I have commanded you. And behold, I am with you always, to the end of the age. (Matthew 28:18–20)

Consider this for a moment with me. Of all the things Jesus could possibly ask His disciples to do as He readies His return to His Father in heaven, He asks them to co-mission with Him by doing for others what He had done for them: make disciple makers. He's not asking for just spiritual maturity but spiritual multiplication! Not just the making of disciples but reproducing disciple makers!

At the end of His journey, in Acts 1, we do not find Jesus ascending into heaven with His fingers crossed hoping His disciples "got the hint" on disciple making. Nor were the disciples, as they watched Him lift into the clouds, wondering among themselves, "What in the world did He mean by making disciples?" The stakes were way too high for that! After all, this was His team who would advance His Kingdom and launch His Church!

Jesus was very intentional about disciple making from the very beginning: who He chose to invest in, what He passed on, and how He went about doing it. In the end, His disciples knew exactly what He had asked them to do. Jesus had so walked in community with them, revealed His character and ways to them, and demonstrated what obedience looked like for them, that His disciple making blueprint thoroughly resided within them!

Now that we've had a look at the aim and the ingredients of disciple making, let's move on to how God changes someone's life to reflect His character, ways, and mission by learning about His process of transformation.

AIMING FOR APPLICATION

1. How have you been discipled around the character, ways, and mission of Jesus? By whom?

2. How many generations deep have you discipled up to this point in your life?

3. What were your takeaways from the five ingredients of disciple making, and how can they help you create a healthy environment in which to make disciples?

CHAPTER 7

The Disciple Maker's Process of Transformation

W hile discipling Pablo, a great young business leader, via *A Discipleship Journey (ADJ)*, I taught him God's process of transformation: *Revelation—Obedience—Transformation*. When God reveals (shows) something to us, and we commit to walk in obedience to what He's revealed, we can anticipate transformation—both in and through our lives! It is a process we see throughout the Scriptures in the lives of people like Moses, Abraham, Joshua, David, Nehemiah, Esther, Mary, Jesus' disciples, Paul—and, of course, in the life of Jesus!

Pablo was self-employed, and his wife, Raquel, was a rising young executive at a Fortune 500 firm. She was on pace to become the youngest Executive Vice-President (EVP) of her company, and things, they thought, were headed in that direction. However, one night, in a time of silent prayer, the Lord revealed to his wife that her name and identity was not EVP, but rather, "Mommy"! At that time, they had a three-year-old little boy, and this impression from the Lord initially felt like a gut punch considering all that Raquel had worked so hard for.

As they had learned to do, together they talked and prayed about this impression. After a particularly intense three-hour time of prayer, Pablo and Raquel realized that God was revealing a part of His destiny for their family. As a couple, they had always asked God for clarity, and here it was! What God was revealing, they set their hearts on obeying! Raquel walked into her office the following Monday and announced her resignation. She finished her job there well, staying on board for a few months until she had both found and trained her replacement.

Pablo and Raquel had come to understand that obeying what Jesus reveals often comes with a cost. But they have also reaped the rewards of obedience as the trajectory of their family has been wonderfully transformed into a cohesive unit that walks and works well together as one to this day!

*****

Transformation.

It's the end game of Jesus' blueprint for disciple making. For individuals, churches, and societies.

Transformation is a change, initiated by God, that when we cooperate with it, advances His Kingdom. Transformation *in* one's life by looking and living more like Jesus, and *through* one's life, by impacting the lives of the people and the world around them, like Jesus.

We see this practically demonstrated in the lives of those Jesus discipled. Among them, Peter moving from fisherman to disciple to denier to "fisher of men." Mary of Magdala, who traveled with the Twelve, moving from healing to herald, being the first to see and declare Jesus alive after the resurrection. Matthew, a looked-down-upon tax collector, moves from the tax booth to traveling and ministering with Jesus for three years, while writing a Gospel that impacts the world still to this day. And what about Thomas, who moves from "doubter" to one who later dies for Jesus as a martyr in India.

Transformation works from the inside out. A life transformed within becomes a vehicle through which transformation travels to impact the lives of others.

In our last chapter, we looked at the aim and ingredients of disciple making. In this one, we'll give our attention to God's process of transformation. To begin, I would like to consider the fruit of the transformational community led by Jesus' disciples in the Book of Acts.

The Book of Acts: A Transformational Community

In Acts 2, following the empowering of the Holy Spirit, and the bold preaching of Peter, the disciples get their first crack at disciple making.

And they devoted themselves to the apostles' teaching and the fellowship, to the breaking of bread and the prayers. And awe came upon every soul, and many wonders and signs were being done through the apostles. And all who believed were together and had all things in common. And they were selling their possessions and belongings and distributing the proceeds to all, as any had need. And day by day, attending the temple together and breaking bread in their homes, they received their food with glad and generous hearts, praising God and having favor with all the people. And the Lord added to their number day by day those who were being saved. (Acts 2:42–47)

This is our first glimpse of the disciples reproducing what Jesus had invested in them. All the same ingredients are in play. Truth being purposely passed on. We see them continuing in community. Expressions of obeying what Jesus had taught. It appears that the disciples continued living just as they had with Jesus, only now including these new disciples in the same kinds of activities and with the same attitude of heart.

These second-generation disciples weren't just being "taught," but like Jesus had done with His Twelve, they were being drawn into a life of godly obedience that was bringing transformation. They were applying what they were learning to their lives. Their new love for and obedience to Jesus was bringing about genuine transformation that began to spread throughout Jerusalem and beyond.

And the word of God continued to increase, and the number of the disciples multiplied greatly in Jerusalem, and a great many of the priests became obedient to the faith. (Acts 6:7)

The Word of God increasing, disciples greatly multiplying, and "a great many" of the priests becoming obedient to the faith! What is emerging here in the Book of Acts, based on the Jesus blueprint, is an incredible transformational community!

A Presence Community

There was a genuine and tangible sense of Jesus being near and with them as they gathered (Acts 2:14); reached out (2:5–41); interacted (5:1–13); and did what Jesus did (5:12–16); even amid persecution (7:54–60).

A Praying Community

They prayed in one accord (Acts 1:14); they were devoted to prayer (2:42); the leadership was committed to prayer (6:4); they prayed through persecution (12:1–17); their prayers launched the missionary movement (13:1–3).

An Empowered Community

God's power was often demonstrated in direct answer to their prayers: believers were emboldened (Acts 4:31); healings and miracles manifested (9:40); vision was imparted (10:9–48); angelic deliverance occurred (12:6–19); a jailor and his family were converted (16:25–34).

An Ever-Expanding Community

The newly formed church continued to grow and be added to (Acts 2:41,48), with men and women coming to Jesus (5:14), not only in Jerusalem (6:7), but also in Judea and Samaria (9:31) and beyond (11:19–26).

A One-Heart, One-Mind Community

They expressed unity by operating in oneness of heart and mind (Acts 1:14), sharing life together (2:42–48), while gladly and generously meeting each other's needs (4:32–34).

An Obeying Jesus Community

They referenced God's ways in the Scriptures (Acts 1:15–26) and did what Jesus had taught them to do, while daily following the lead of the Holy Spirit (8:26–40; 10:9–48).

A Fear of the Lord Community

A sense of awe fell upon them (Acts 2:43) as they reverenced God above all else (5:1–13), walking in the Fear of the Lord (9:11), and not giving in to the fear of man (5:29).

A Missional Community

This band of Jesus followers continued to extend His Kingdom from Jerusalem to the ends of the earth (Acts 13–28).

A Society Impacting Community

Along with "turning the world upside down" (Acts 17:6), meeting the needs of the needy (4:34–35; 11:27–29) and healing the sick (5:16; 8:7; 9:34), the disciples participated in relational transformation between Jews and Gentiles (15:1–35).

A Sacrificial, Enduring Community

The disciples endured great persecution (Acts 4:1–31; 5:17–42), as Jesus had said they would; this was soon followed by the deaths of Stephen (6:8–8:1) and James (12:1–3) and the imprisonments of Peter (12:6–19) and Paul (16:16–40; 24:26–27; 28:17–31).

A Jesus-Glorifying Community

The name of Jesus was exalted (Acts 2:21; 3:15–17; 4:10; 5:39–41) and glorified through the lives and sacrifices of His disciples (7:55–56; 11:15–18; 12:21–24; 13:46–49; 21:17–20).

A Disciple Making Community

Their mission was to simply obey the mandate Jesus gave them to make disciple makers, and they multiplied greatly (Acts 2:42–47; 5:42; 6:7; 15:35; 18:11; 28:31).

This is the fruit of the ingredients of the Jesus blueprint of disciple making! What Jesus follower wouldn't love being a part of a community like this—and what pastor wouldn't love leading one? Talk about generational impact!

The Acts of the Discipled

While here in the Book of Acts, I would like to share several observations about disciple making that I have gleaned from it over the years.

First, I've come to realize that the Book of Acts is not really the Book of Acts because of the coming of the Holy Spirit. Acts is Acts because of the coming of the Holy Spirit on discipled people! Three years of deliberate discipling by Jesus infused by the power of the Holy Spirit provides an accurate picture of why Acts is what it is. I like referring to Acts as "The Acts of the Discipled."

Second, we learn from Acts that first-generation disciples were intent on obeying the Matthew 28:18-20 commission of Jesus to "make disciples." Their primary focus was not winning converts, planting churches, or impacting society. Rather, they cultivated disciple-making communities wherever they went, in obedience to Jesus, and the *by-product* (or fruit) was many people won to Jesus, lots of churches planted, and a changed society! Because they had personally experienced being a part of a disciple making community with Jesus for three years, they (super)naturally reproduced them!

Third, the primary existence of a church was to serve as a "disciple making hub." It functioned as a "spiritual hothouse" where disciples of Jesus were reproduced. They grew to reflect His character, were developed to reference His ways, and were equipped to participate in His mission. We see this not only in Jerusalem, but also in Antioch, and in the various cities Paul visits, where he later continues to disciple through his letters.

And, fourth, the goal of the disciples was reproducing disciple makers. Through Jesus, and their obedience to do the same, was launched a reproducible disciple making movement. The seed that had been planted in them by Jesus, when fully grown, would produce more reproducible seeds that were to multiply disciple makers for generations to come. Like that first generation of disciple makers, each generation needs to "own" their generation by taking responsibility to disciple those who are currently on the planet with them—among every tribe, tongue, people, and nation.

The Process

A few years ago, I received an invitation to lunch with a pastor who I had not yet met. As we were seated in the restaurant, we began to chat about family and other common areas of interest. I could tell we were on the way to becoming fast friends!

He was aware that I lead an organization whose aim is making disciple makers within the church and among societal leaders. He sensed that I knew something about transformation taking hold in the lives of followers of Jesus. He said, "Dave, I come from a denomination in the Body of Christ where the Scriptures are highly valued and studied. The people I pastor know the Word. They could provide you with overviews and highlights from books of the Bible..." At that moment, with his glasses lowered to the edge of his nose, he leaned across the table toward me and with great humility and the sincere concern of a shepherd who loves his flock, he stated, "...but I'm not seeing them be transformed!"

Pause. Take a moment to really consider what he's saying, "My people know the Scriptures… but I'm not seeing them be transformed!" Obviously, he wasn't commenting on the transforming power of the Scriptures! Instead, he was seeking how to make sure the Scriptures take hold of people so they are transformed more into the likeness of Jesus.

As our conversation continued, I shared with him God's process of transformation. I see God using this process in people's lives all throughout the Scriptures. I wanted to draw a diagram to explain this to him, so with my finger, I drew three imaginary connected circles on the table to explain this to him. I labeled the last circle *Transformation*, as that was his target.

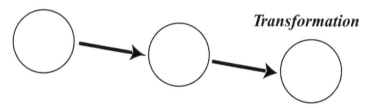

I offered a little of what I've learned about transformation over the years. The more we behold God's character and ways, the more the Holy Spirit transforms us into His likeness.

And we all, with unveiled face, beholding the glory of the Lord, are being transformed into the same image from one degree of glory to another. For this comes from the Lord who is the Spirit. (2 Corinthians 3:18)

Transformation is something that God does! It's His intervening in our lives to bring His life to bear upon us, our relationships, and communities. We, as human beings, cannot make spiritual transformation happen. Because of my love for people, I wish I could, but it is a divine work of God. Like an apple seed, the actual transformation from seed to tree to fruit to orchard(s) belongs to God. He is the sole source of spiritual transformation!

Back at our table diagram, we began to tackle the starting place, *Revelation*. I'm not talking about the last book in our Bibles, but rather, how God reveals things to us. It's how we came to Jesus in the first place: He allowed us to spiritually perceive our desperate condition and His offer of love, forgiveness, and reconciliation. Revelation is the parting of curtains so we see as God sees.

Revelation

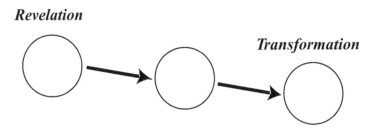

Transformation

Let me illustrate. Imagine yourself in a theater. Perhaps you're there to watch a family member perform as part of a play. You hear the noise of the gathering crowd while you pick out your seat. The lights dim, and your attention focuses on those huge velvety curtains in front of you. You have no idea what's behind that curtain. As the curtain pulls back, you have a completely different vantage point as you see the dusty streets of an old western town! What you could not see only seconds before you now can see! That's "revelation"!

Consider the scene in Matthew 16 where Jesus asks His disciples who people think He is. Some think He's John the Baptist, Elijah, Jeremiah, or one of the prophets come back to life. Then He asks them what they think. Peter pipes up and says, "You are the Christ, the Son of the Living God!" Hear afresh these words of Jesus in verse 17:

> *And Jesus answered him, "Blessed are you, Simon Bar-Jonah! For flesh and blood has not revealed this to you, but my Father who is in heaven."*

Like transformation, revelation is sourced in God alone. He is the Revealer. If He doesn't part the curtains, we have a hard time seeing where He's leading our lives. The good news is that we can posture ourselves to receive revelation: seeking His face in worship, prayer, and the Scriptures, through a sermon, or in a conversation. When I can't yet see something from God, I can ask Him for revelation on it!

Information and revelation are two very different things. Information provides us with knowledge, facts, and figures. It may inform, but by itself, it doesn't transform. On the other hand, revelation leads to heart and life transformation! When God reveals something to us, He "pulls back the curtains" to allow us to see His truth, pointing us to respond to what He's revealing.

So, in this process, God is doing the "heavy lifting," both revealing and transforming! What is our role in this? Our response is obedience.

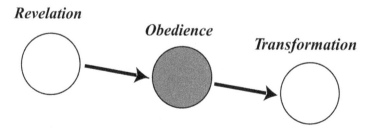

The life of Jesus revolved around obeying His Father. We see just how central obedience was to Jesus in John 5:19 when we read, *The Son can do nothing of his own accord, but only what He sees the Father doing. For whatever the Father does, that the Son does likewise.* Also, at one of the most intense moments of His life, in Gethsemane, Jesus remained obedient, fully yielding to His Father's will (Matthew 26:39).

Fueled by our great love for Jesus, we are to walk daily in obedience, doing what Jesus has revealed to us to do. When God reveals something to us, it's not meant to be negotiated; it's meant to be obeyed! As stated before, obedience is the engine of transformation! God reveals something to us; we obey Him out of love and trust; He brings the transformation—both in and through our lives!

Our Reference Points

Over the last couple chapters, we've covered some good pieces on Jesus' blueprint of disciple making. We have considered our *aim* by defining disciple making, observed the *ingredients*, and discovered God's amazing *process* of transformation.

There's another important piece that needs to be added to our blueprint blend as we get more hands-on: our reference points.

What the Scriptures teach
What the life of Jesus models
Following the lead of the Holy Spirit

We must be scriptural in all that we do. It is our divine plumb line regarding God's character, ways, and mission. Without a "scriptural tether point," viewed through the whole counsel of Scripture, there is no solid footing or spiritual authority to stand on.

The truths we walk in and disciple others with must be grounded in the truth of Scripture. A good question for both disciple maker and the one being discipled is, "Where is this tethered in Scripture?"

Now, we all know people who can quote Scripture like crazy, but the way they live their lives does not reflect Jesus at all! We need a working knowledge of the Scriptures that focuses on loving and obeying Jesus in our daily lives—that's what brings about genuine transformation of the heart!

The life of Jesus, as seen in the Scriptures, is a second reference point for us. His words, how He lived His life, related to people, walked in obedience to His Father, trusted the lead of the Holy Spirit in His life, etc., are things we need to be familiar with as disciple makers. Jesus is also the Master Disciple Maker! If we want to be effective transformational and generational disciple makers, we have much to learn from Jesus! A periodic read-through of the four Gospels freshens up this reference point in our hearts and minds.

Our third essential reference point is following the lead of the Holy Spirit. Without question, the Holy Spirit is the key player in our discipling relationships! He knows where and how to transform a person's heart to be more like Jesus. He knows their life journey inside out. He knows their strengths and gifts, their weaknesses and vulnerabilities. He knows their destiny and the people He wants to add to their life for help along the way. He's the One who empowers them to live a godly life, to serve Jesus and others. He knows how to uniquely shape them around God's character, ways, and mission. He is the one leading the process of transformation!

In our next chapter, we'll consider practical tools that will equip you to engage in becoming both an effective and fruitful disciple maker!

AIMING FOR APPLICATION

1. What did you observe about the fruit of Jesus' disciple making in the Church in Acts?

2. Take a few minutes now and put into practice the Process of Transformation. What was revelational to you from this chapter? How might you obey that in your life?

3. Which of the three Reference Points do you tend to refer to the most? How about least?

CHAPTER 8

The Disciple Maker's Tools

While hosting a disciple making gathering some years ago, I had the privilege of visiting with a wise veteran of disciple making, Dr. John Tolson. John has served as a faith developer for some of our nation's leading executives and athletes and has impacted the lives of thousands through his discipling, speaking, and resources. As we were visiting, he asked me,

Do you know the number one reason why people who know they should be making disciples, don't do it?

After acknowledging to him that I didn't know, he replied,

The greatest reason why disciple making doesn't happen is very practical. If someone isn't discipled in the Scriptures with a tool they've walked through and applied in their own lives, they will not feel confident in discipling others.

One of the privileges my team and I have is launching people into disciple making. We do so by using the Scriptures and, as John suggested, providing a tool they can walk through that they can then use effectively to disciple others. Our tool, *A Discipleship Journey (ADJ),* is a scripturally sound, proven, and practical one that we've served many locally, nationally, and globally. It points disciples to Jesus and the Scriptures while helping them in a relational setting to obey and apply into their lives the truths the Holy Spirit is revealing to them.

Grant, a media influencer I was walking alongside, decided it was time for him to launch his own *ADJ* group. So, we talked. Between the things that I had in my heart and the great questions he asked, we settled on four reference points to help him get started.

First, Grant needed to figure out *who* he should be discipling. I shared with him the question I always begin with, "In whose ears are your words big?" In other words, who has God already given you favor with, where your life and words have weight in their lives? This proved to be valuable to him as he sorted out who God was leading him to invite into his *ADJ* group.

Second, we reviewed the process of transformation: *Revelation—Obedience—Transformation.* This process is facilitated by two questions, "What has the Holy Spirit revealed to you?" and "How are you going to obey this in our life?" These are the keys to making sure what God is revealing to those you are discipling is being practically applied to their lives. Without this process, they'll end up only informed and not transformed! Grant was totally tracking with me.

Third, we talked about how to disciple each person individually while still maintaining a small group setting. With the focus being on real-life application versus a broad discussion used by many Bible studies and small groups in church life, you can make a more personal and significant investment in each person. Of course, conversations beyond group time naturally occur and are equally important. Again, Grant was following where I was leading.

And fourth, I reminded him that he needs to share with his group upfront that once they finish their *ADJ* experience, he expects them to multiply by launching their own disciple making groups! This journey isn't just for their personal spiritual development; it is so they can also actively participate in Jesus' Great Co-Mission, reproducing what they've applied in those whom God brings into their lives, who can then do the same for others!

Over the last few years, Grant has done a great job of applying these four reference points as he reproduces disciples!

*****

Clarify—Identify—Multiply

When helping people launch disciple making in their lives, I've pointed them to three practical things they can do to get off on the right foot: *Clarify—Identify—Multiply*. As we look at each of these, please don't make this "theory," but rather make it real in your life where you are living today. How might this apply to discipling within your relationships and vocation? Pay attention to the nudges of the Holy Spirit within you as we navigate our way through these three launch points.

Clarify

There are several things you need to clarify as you begin your journey as a disciple maker:

- Your commitment
- Your priorities
- Your time

If you just add "making disciples" to your to-do list or throw it in the mix with everything else you are doing in life, it won't happen. We must remember going into this that if this is God's divine plan, expressed through the blueprint of Jesus, the devil will do everything he can to hinder you from becoming an effective and fruitful disciple maker! I've watched this happen many times over many years. Don't kid yourself; this will take genuine commitment on your part.

Without a revelation from the Scriptures by the Holy Spirit to your heart of the centrality of Jesus' disciple-making mandate, you won't gain any real traction! You must see it like Jesus sees it. You must be utterly, unreservedly, and wholeheartedly convinced that part of your calling in life—as is true with every follower of Jesus—is to be a reproducible disciple maker.

Jesus' primary thrust was investing in the Twelve. He didn't allow the pull of the crowds, the opinions of the religious leaders, or the side-tracking attempts of Satan to draw Him away from making disciple makers. What might Satan use to draw you away from this new commitment?

Our priorities in life emerge out of what we value or deem as most important to us. Now valuing obedience to Jesus as a disciple maker, we need to practically consider changes in our thinking, attitudes, and actions. How will this new priority affect what you've currently been doing? How does it impact the way you view and relate to those around you? How does this affect your time and calendar? Where might you need to adjust or what will you need to take off your plate?

Right there, next to loving Jesus and our neighbor (the Great Commandment), disciple making is to be our primary mission, wherever He's appointed us to serve. It's what Jesus co-missioned His followers to do with Him. It means making a commitment and prioritizing your time, calendar, and relationships around it.

Identify

Once you've made a commitment and adjusted your priorities to engage in Jesus' disciple making mandate, it's time to start asking "who should I disciple?"

A disciple maker is somebody who is a step or two ahead of another who needs to grow. They are not perfect, an "expert in their field," or even spiritually fully grown themselves. They are, however, a step or two ahead and willing to invest what Jesus has given them in others.

So, who are you to disciple?

Begin by looking at your current God-given sphere of relationships. Who are followers of Jesus that need to be discipled in your family, among your friends and neighbors, and within your vocation? These are people Jesus has already brought into your life.

You might be thinking, "That's great, but how do I narrow this group down?" That's a good question! Let me share with you the grid I look through.

First, I like asking the question my friend David Shirk once asked me many years ago:

In whose ears are your words big?

Have you noticed that, with some people, your words carry the weight of a feather, while others weight your words like gold? I've learned that when you find someone who responds to your words, it's important to note that Jesus may be giving you a clue that this is someone He desires for you to consider investing in. Expressions of unusual favor and receptivity help you identify God-ordained heart-links that make it easy for you to give and for them to receive.

> Getting Practical: Make a list of those in your life today in whose ears your words are big. This is your "pool of possibilities" you can begin to prayerfully and practically wade through.

Next, I use the acronym F.A.S.T. to help me discern the current condition of those in my possibility pool to determine if they are ripe for disciple making. I'm talking about the qualities of faithfulness, availability, servant-heartedness, and teachability. I'm willing to give my best efforts and time to make disciples, but I also want to make sure they are really "hungry of heart" and ready to run with me.

Faithfulness speaks of one's character. If they are invited into my disciple making group, and say "I'm in," can I count on them being there? *Availability* represents their time and getting it on their calendar, making it a priority in their life. *Servant-heartedness* shows a desire to take what they are being given to bless and invest in the lives of others. *Teachability* is an attitude of heart, reflecting humility, and a willingness to learn and apply what the Holy Spirit is revealing in their life.

<u>Getting Practical</u>: So, looking at your "pool of possibilities," who on that list are the "hungry of heart," the faithful, available, servant-hearted, and teachable?

Once I've taken things this far, it's time for me to spend time seeking Jesus about who He is giving me the "green light" to pour into. Because Jesus spent the whole night praying about who He was to disciple (Luke 6:12–16), I want to give myself to purposeful prayer about this as well. I want to spend my time where it will bear the most fruit for His Kingdom purposes, and Jesus knows best who needs what He's poured into me. Sometimes my "obvious" choices are not His! Because I want to obey Him, I stay dependent on His leading and guiding my life.

<u>Getting Practical</u>: When will you set aside time to seek the Lord about those you've narrowed down on your list? Who is He confirming that you are to invite to join you on a discipleship journey?

Once I know who the Lord would have me invest in, and I've asked them to pray about it, I like to gather them to have a conversation together about the why, where, when, what, and how of our disciple making group. This is my final process to confirm who is in and who is not in a place to participate. It's during this time that I like to eyeball each one and ask, "Are you willing to match my commitment?" In other words, if I commit a certain amount of time and effort to disciple them, are they equally committed to follow through with what they've committed to? If they can't, I'll still love them, pray for them, help them, and enjoy their company—but I won't disciple them.

Disciple making is different than friendship, mentoring, being in a small group, or even pastoring someone. Based on Jesus and how He related to the Twelve, disciple making has a higher bar of commitment. In the story of the rich young ruler in Mark 10:17–31, Jesus converses with him about eternal life. He then invites him to sell what he had, give it to the poor, and follow Him. Disheartened, this young man turns and walks away. Even though Jesus loved him (verse 21), he didn't lower the discipleship bar or chase him down; rather he let him walk away. Disciple making that involves the constant "chasing down" of people will wear you down. However, engaging with those willing to be committed will result in good fruit!

> Getting Practical: When you ask, "Are you willing to match my commitment?" who looked you in the eyes and answered, "I'm all in!"? Those are the ones ready to be discipled!

Two other quick things.

You might ask, "How many should I disciple at a time?" That's a great question! Jesus discipled a dozen at a time, but that may not be best for us or those we are discipling. Some will tell you that one-on-one is the way to go, others like smaller groups of two to four, and some prefer larger groups of eight to twelve. I've found that a lot depends on the disciple maker's time and gifts and what resources are being used. In the end, it needs to be effective and fruitful in the ones being discipled. Wisdom dictates to start small, experiment with it a bit, and find what works best for you.

Should men disciple men and women disciple women? As a norm, yes. However, when I host Lionshare's annual leadership disciple making expression, *A Leadership Journey*, we do it as a group of around twelve to fifteen people, so I allow both men and women to participate. The key is always to be wise and listen when your spouse tells you they aren't good with it.

Multiply

When you get to this point, it means you've clarified your commitment to disciple making and have identified those you will be discipling. That's great! Now come the fun part and the work: reproducing the character, ways, and mission of Jesus in them so they can become part of the multiplication process as well!

As you begin your group, it needs to be clearly communicated and understood from the get-go that your expectations are that those you're discipling are there to grow and mature in the Lord and to become effective and fruitful disciple makers themselves! Yes, that's right, they are expected—in due time—to multiply what's been given to them in the lives of others.

Disciple making math is not addition, it is multiplication! Because each one who is discipled is to also reproduce disciples, the increase happens in leaps and bounds. Let me illustrate this for you.

Imagine if you started with fifty people who were committed to disciple two people each for one year to the point where they are ready to be disciple makers. At the end of year one, you'd now have 150 disciple makers, the original fifty, plus the 100 they discipled. Then, those same 150 commit to disciple two over another year. At the end of the second year we've got 450 disciple makers. Maybe not a big deal but take a look at the incredible rate of multiplication that occurs if this is repeated each year over a span of less than two decades!

End of Year Total Disciple Makers

1	150	10	2,952,450
2	450	11	8,857,350
3	1,350	12	26,572,050
4	4,050	13	79,716,150
5	12,150	14	239,148,450
6	36,450	15	717,445,350
7	109,350	16	2,152,336,050
8	328,050	17	6,457,008,150
9	984,150	18	19,371,024,450

From the original fifty who are committed to discipling two per year, there are nearly 3,000,000 disciple makers after the first decade! Then, the rate begins to explode exponentially! According to the United Nations, the 2050 population is estimated to reach 9.8 billion.[1] This disciple making math helps us see how we really can disciple the world! Even after the passing of centuries, never has man devised a better plan to impact the entire world than the blueprint of Jesus!

Are you committed to do your part in this by discipling at least two people each year?

Teach—Demonstrate—Replicate

Several chapters back, I mentioned how Jesus passed things on to others via the method of *teach—demonstrate—replicate*. He taught to the point of understanding, while demonstrating what it practically looked like, and then He asked His disciples to replicate it in front of Him.

Think for a moment of how often you've been given something to do, yet you didn't really understand it yourself. Or, how often you had to figure something out on your own because no one ever taught or modeled it for you? Now—this gets a little scary—consider how often you've done this same thing to others!

Jesus' blueprint for passing things on and fanning the flames of disciple maker multiplication is:

Teach—Demonstrate—Replicate

This needs to become every disciple maker's refrain! It needs to serve as the disciple maker's compass. If you want someone to really catch the character, ways, and mission of Jesus, you must teach—demonstrate—replicate!

Teach

Teach is communicating a truth in such a way that the person you are discipling relates to it, understands it, and grasps how it can be applied to their life in obedience to Jesus.

Demonstrate

Demonstrate is the modeling of that truth—or the show-me-what-it-looks-like aspect of Jesus' blueprint. It's what gives the truth taught real credibility and authority—seeing it displayed in another's life right before our very eyes.

Replicate

Once disciples fully understand and see truth via teaching and demonstrating, it is their turn to replicate it in front of you. It's their opportunity to show you what they've learned and received and your opportunity to coach them up by guiding and encouraging them.

I've applied this as a dad, leader, disciple maker, and even as a football coach. When coaching high school football, this became the primary method I used to help our guys grasp what it meant to be good tacklers.

I had the opportunity to brush up on a tackling technique, "hit, wrap and drive," by participating in an NFL/NFF Coaching Academy hosted for high school coaches by the coaching staff of our hometown team, the Tennessee Titans. "Hit" meant placing one's facemask in the numbers of the ball carrier. "Wrap" represented the position of a tackler's arms around the ball carrier's waist with one hand being locked around the other arm's wrist. "Drive" was used to describe the movement and momentum of the back leg thrusting forward to stop the runner in his tracks. After learning this, "hit, wrap, and drive," became a regular part of our afternoon practices.

When one of our defensive players was not tackling correctly I would apply the *teach—demonstrate—replicate* method right then and there. First, I would pull him aside privately to remind and reteach the player the "hit, wrap, and drive" technique. In the process, I would demonstrate for him what each part of it was to look like. I would then return him to his position during practice where I would have him replicate what he had learned in front of me on the field of play, allowing me to guide, tweak, and encourage him. It worked, and we soon became known league wide as a tremendous tackling team. Our success in this area helped contribute to a league championship.

Think about how this method applies in your life at home, in your vocation, and in church life. Consider the ramifications in the lives of your children—physically, relationally or spiritually—if you take the time and make the effort to *teach—demonstrate—replicate*!

Disciple Making Cornerstones

When talking about disciple making, I find that most people think that means helping others grow in one's walk with God. And, that would be correct! However, most folks often don't realize that there are various expressions of and purposes for being spiritually developed.

Within Lionshare, we have what we refer to as our *Disciple Making Cornerstones*, four integrated and distinct expressions of making disciples. Before breaking this down a bit, take a moment and give this diagram a quick look, beginning with foundational disciple making and moving clockwise.

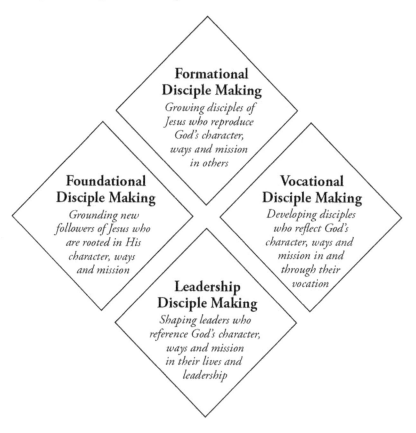

Formational Disciple Making
Growing disciples of Jesus who reproduce God's character, ways and mission in others

Foundational Disciple Making
Grounding new followers of Jesus who are rooted in His character, ways and mission

Vocational Disciple Making
Developing disciples who reflect God's character, ways and mission in and through their vocation

Leadership Disciple Making
Shaping leaders who reference God's character, ways and mission in their lives and leadership

When someone gives their life to Jesus, we need to help get them grounded right away in some basic foundations of God's Kingdom. These "new babies in the Lord" need some extra tending as they are rooted in forgiveness, discover God's character, the Scriptures, God's family (the Church), His mission, etc. Referencing our friend, Grant Edwards[2], we call this *foundational disciple making.*

Ideally, building on a good foundation, *formational disciple making* focuses on disciples growing and experiencing more of God's character, ways, and mission, being formed more in the image of Jesus. They acquire a working knowledge of the Scriptures, how to follow the lead of the Holy Spirit, how to relate well with others, how to share their faith, etc. This results in spiritual maturity, fruitfulness, and the ability to reproduce the life of Jesus (making disciple makers) in others.

Usually during the ongoing formational process, *vocational disciple making* is added into the mix. The focus here is on developing seasoned disciples who reflect God's character and the wisdom of His ways, in and through their vocation. They also are equipped to co-mission with Jesus to effectively reproduce the same within other disciples within their vocation.

Leadership disciple making shapes maturing disciples to reference God's character, ways, and mission as they lead in their homes, vocations, churches, and community. This includes personal wholeness, godly character, servant leadership, leading out of relationship, hearing from God, creating cultures of honor, being a leader others will follow, spiritual warfare, margin, finishing well, etc.

There are numerous "investing-in-others" terms that we commonly use in our culture today, like mentoring and coaching. I want to be clear that disciple making is always about developing disciples of Jesus around His character, ways, and mission. There is always a scriptural component to it. Mentoring, which is passing something on that one has to another, and coaching, which is strategically guiding someone toward a discovered end, can certainly be methods used to impart the ways of God. It depends, of course, on who the mentor or coach is.

The key thing to note here is that disciple making *always* references God's character, ways, and mission via the Scriptures as its source for shaping and guiding lives. At its core, that is what makes it different than mentoring or coaching, and why the pieces in our cornerstones of vocational and leadership disciple making can be unique.

Vocational Focal Points

While applying these practices and principles within each of the four cornerstones, there are other pieces I add when discipling people in the ways of God related to their vocation. After all, businesspeople need different development than those who serve in the arts and sports. Government leaders require shaping that is unique to what they do, as do those in science, the media, education, and every other vocational field. Over the years, I have found these five focal points helpful while walking alongside and discipling those within their vocation.

1. Calling

Calling references both a person's internal "wiring" and God-given abilities, as well as their obedience to God's leading in their life regarding where He has appointed them to serve for His purposes within society.

2. Character

One of the greatest ways to reveal God is through consistent godly character. Because every vocational field has its own challenges, enticements, and pitfalls, disciples of Jesus need to be aware of where they may be tested and where they need to be strengthened in character. For example, counteracting an environment of greed will require a greater deposit of generosity. Those called to entertainment, where vanity and pride tend to flourish, will need to cultivate a humble spirit.

3. Competency

The Scriptures teach that we should offer our very best to those we serve and lead (Ephesians 6: 5–9). When working within our vocations, disciples of Jesus must take opportunities to be shaped and equipped to excel in serving others better at every level in their field. The disciple's aim isn't on competing with others to "be the best" but is instead in giving everything you have "unto the Lord" so that His reputation is enhanced and people's lives are bettered and blessed!

4. Connecting

One of the greatest strengths of a disciple of Jesus should be the way they relate to the people around them: staff, employers, employees, partners, boards, clients, customers, vendors, members, and others. Being discipled to relate well builds good teams, creates cultures of mutual honor and respect, and benefits the communities we have the privilege of influencing.

5. Commitment

Whether committing to a company, project, program, ministry, team or mission, a disciple's commitment will be tested. Disciples can benefit those they work with when the qualities of faithfulness, endurance, a stellar attitude, a unifying spirit, and finishing well in all that they put their hands to are evident.

Alright, I've given you some practical handles to launch disciple making in your relationships and/or within your vocation! If you apply these things, you'll find yourself launching and leading an effective and fruitful expression of disciple making!

AIMING FOR APPLICATION

1. As you look around in your relationships and vocation, "in whose ears are your words big"? Who are the "hungry of heart" around you?

2. What can you currently *teach—demonstrate—replicate* related to vocational disciple making: calling, character, connecting, competencies, and commitment?

3. What stood out to you the most as you looked over the four disciple making cornerstones?

4. What are the next steps you can begin to take to launch into disciple making? Make sure you visit www.Lionshare.org to gain further insights and get practical resources to enable you to launch out as an effective and fruitful disciple maker!

CHAPTER 9

More Vocational Disciple Making Stories

W e've covered a lot of ground regarding Jesus' blueprint of disciple making. To freshen it up a bit and see all the pieces together, let's do a quick review of what we've learned.

- Our *aim* is reproducing the character, ways, and mission of Jesus in those around us, expecting them to multiply the same in others.
- The *ingredients* are a context of relational community, replacing false beliefs by teaching the truth of Scripture, creating a culture—or norm—of obeying what Jesus is

revealing in our lives, and helping those you're discipling to find other followers of Jesus to reproduce within.

- The *process of transformation* cultivates an attentiveness within those you are discipling to what God is revealing to them, as you come alongside of them to help them walk in that obedience, while trusting God for transformation, whether in them or through them.

- Our *reference points* of the Scriptures, the life of Jesus, and the leading of the Holy Spirit are there to serve us well.

- The *tools* of clarify, identify, and multiply are there to help us be personally prepared, discover who you are to disciple, and how to go about doing it. *Teach—demonstrate— replicate* is a practical way of guiding people toward obeying Jesus. ·

- The *Disciple Making Cornerstones* allow us to disciple people around God's character, ways, and mission where they are at in their journey with Jesus. *Vocational disciple making* specifically focuses on developing disciples serving within your vocational field in God's ways in their calling, character, competencies, connecting, and commitment.

Vocational Disciple Making Stories

To both encourage and envision you for vocational disciple making, I'd like to share with you some more stories from my journey. Like all the others, these stories are all real and true (although their names have been changed) and are about friends I have had the joy and privilege of walking alongside for a season in a discipling relationship. They all reference applying aspects of God's character, ways, and mission within people's lives and vocations.

I trust their stories will continue to inspire you to connect your vocation with disciple making, understanding afresh the difference that you can make in a person's life and in society. Doing so advances God's Kingdom, betters and blesses the lives of people, and glorifies the name of Jesus.

*****

Hal: The Honorable Team Leader

While chatting one day about life, family, and the latest sports stories, my businessman buddy Hal asked me, "How does a godly Team Leader go about releasing people from their jobs?" Hal had received word that week that the higher-ups in his company were requiring him to let two of his team go. He clearly knew that leaving a pink slip on their desks and requiring these faithful team members to pack up and "be out by noon" was not the way to handle it. He also knew that well-used phrase, "it's not personal, it's business" wouldn't cut it either.

Hal was working in the corporate world where numbers, profit, and hitting sales targets are a way of life. It is a world where the norm is focusing more on the result versus the individual who is doing the work to hit corporate objectives. I was glad to see that, despite his corporate environment, Hal was trying to implement the ways of God as a leader!

This led us to a conversation around Romans 12:10, "outdo one another in showing honor." As a godly leader in any vocational field, we are to do our best to honor those we work with. Honor has to do with recognizing a person's value in who they are, what they bring to the table, and what they accomplish. Hal grabbed a hold of this scriptural principle and ran with it!

He met with each of the two people individually that he needed to release, sharing his heart and what it was that he needed to do. Hal also rallied his team to allow them the opportunity to affirm them and express their appreciation for their years of service. He wrote letters of recommendation for them to use as they were pursuing their next jobs and made sure they had some severance to take care of them while they made the transition. They thanked Hal for being "real" with them and making them feel as good as possible under tough circumstances.

Not only did Hal handle this situation with honor, but it also spilled over to his leadership of his team. He began to make sure that each person understood his or her value to both him and the corporation. He was amazed to learn from some who had worked there for over twenty years that nobody had ever told them how valuable and appreciated they were for what they did!

Hal made it a practice to honor his team via encouragement, praise, and recognition. Occasional salary bumps helped too! He also coached his team to realize that if they treated the individuals they worked with at other companies in the same way, it created a better working environment for them and their clients, which often enabled them to realize their corporate objectives as well!

*****

Cam: The Non-Initiating Pastor

When I ran our Acts Alive Youth Discipleship Camps, I had the privilege of meeting Cameron, a youth pastor who would become both a friend and someone I would deeply and deliberately invest in. Following his years working with teenagers, Cam took on a different role in another city, closer to his roots. He was finding real fruitfulness there discipling people, preaching and teaching, and giving oversight to one of the campuses in a multi-site local church expression.

Over the last several years, Cam was sensing that God was doing something different in his life. He loved his current vocation, but was a bit unsettled and, at times, even wrestling with some frustrations in his role. He remembered a lesson I had learned and shared many times: *what God initiates, He permeates; what I initiate, I have to sustain.* As a godly man, Cam didn't want to initiate anything. He fasted and prayed and sought out godly counsel from spiritual leaders and friends. He continued to allow his heart to dream but wisely chose not to initiate anything. He desired to follow the Lord's lead.

One afternoon, he learned that the person serving in the position within his church, a role he had quietly had his eye on, was moving out of state to take a new role in another organization. An email stated that if anyone wanted to apply for the position that they should talk with their direct supervisor before applying. So, Cam did! It was a dream role for him, and after the conversation with his supervisor, he walked through the process. Eventually, he was selected and accepted the position!

However, God had something else in mind, in addition to his new role! A few months into it, he was in a conversation with someone he had been discipling who plays professional football. He mentioned to Cam that his team did not have a team chaplain (or team pastor). A lunch was initiated for him to meet with the player's head coach, and through the process, God opened the door for Cam to serve as the team chaplain while continuing in his other new role. This was an even bigger dream than he could have ever imagined!

Throughout this process, Cam, and his wife, Samantha, have experienced firsthand the principle *what God initiates, He permeates.* Because God initiated these opportunities and roles, they are confident as a couple about what God has called them to do vocationally, and that He will permeate everything He's led them to do with everything they need to do it. They also can completely trust God no matter what happens, because they know that He's the one who initiated it!

*****

Alexis: The Perplexed Professional

A number of years ago, I met Alexis, a young woman who was part of a church that I have had the privilege of coming alongside. She was bright, talented, had a wonderful personality, and was always hungry to know God more deeply, grow more spiritually and serve others more effectively! Alexis had a vision for, and the matching skillsets, to be a mentor to many. She also was a gifted public communicator. Over time we developed a trusted friendship, and when she began to invite me to speak into her life, I set my heart to be an encouragement to her as a disciple maker.

Because of her many talents, Alexis had many vocational opportunities coming her way, from all kinds of places. Alexis is prone to indecisiveness, so she tends to never meet an opportunity she doesn't like! However, this filled her with anxiety, resulting in frustration, confusion, and an emotional downward spiral that impacted her confidence. To the world around her, Alexis looked like she "had it all together," but she was finding it difficult to hit her stride. She desired focus and peace but instead felt like she was on a vocational merry-go-round.

Alexis reached out to me in the midst of her life's swirl, and we chatted. Actually, she talked, and I did a lot of listening. Answers are not what she needed first and foremost; instead, she just needed me to be "with her" in her confusion by listening well and helping her sort through the heart of the matter—by intentionally pointing her to Jesus. As we referenced Jesus' presence and His ways from the Scriptures, Alexis took ownership of her deep-seated fears of missing God's call, making a wrong decision, and living an unfulfilled life. I did my best to create a non-judgmental space for her to "just be" while she was "becoming," not trying to "fix" her but rather to simply love and listen to her, while also keeping an ear open to the Holy Spirit. This seemed to help clear the clutter and opened a pathway for her to listen to God's direction.

Here is how Alexis put it in her own words:

> *A journey alongside a godly guide helped me bring my anxieties to the cross, which has brought me both life and freedom. A disciple maker who can keep in step with what the Holy Spirit is doing and what the disciple is saying has mastered a skill that is foundational to vocational discernment. It is a holy task to listen and allow the Holy Spirit to lead. Since those days of downward spiraling, I'm learning to lean into peace as I resolve which vocational opportunities are best aligned with my God-given gifts and call.*

Disciple making isn't always about talking. It is often about listening to the one you are pouring your life into and to the wonderful guidance of the Holy Spirit that lives within us!

*****

Travis: The Compassionate CEO

I was invited to breakfast by a young business leader that I was walking alongside. He wanted to introduce me to Travis, a friend of his, and someone he felt I might be able to disciple in life and leadership. Travis and I struck up a relationship that led to him becoming my friend, while also participating in my six-month leadership discipleship intensive, *A Leadership Journey (ALJ)*.

As we walked together, I noticed just how talented Travis was in his knowledge of the Scriptures and in his business acumen. I also noticed what I would call a "sharp edge" within his personality, a place where I believed God wanted to soften him. It was in the way he related with others. Because Travis viewed life very black and white, he could get lost in the grey areas—those places within relationships requiring more tenderness, sensitivity, and nuancing.

As we chatted about this over time, Travis told me that it wasn't that he didn't want to know how to empathize with others, it just wasn't modeled for him while growing up in his home, and no one had ever taken the time to teach or show him what it truly looked like.

As only the Lord can do, He provided an opportunity for this new muscle that he was discovering to grow. While leading his company through a rough patch, Travis learned that one of his team members was dying of cancer. Through this, God began to reveal to him His character attribute of compassion. Talk about an eye-opener for Travis!

Because of a living example that modeled empathy and vulnerability for him, along with the scriptural conversations around compassion that they had, Travis began to change from the inside out. Instead of expressing things in a way that tended to be more cold and matter of fact, he communicated great care and concern among his team as they all wrestled with the loss of their teammate and friend. Travis realized what they needed most was a compassionate leader, and prior to this, he simply didn't know how to show or convey it to those around him. But now, because of his own heart transformation, God was able to express

His character of compassion through him in a wonderful way to provide his team exactly what they needed most!

Not only did this impact his company but living in a more vulnerable and understanding way with others has had a huge and powerful impact on Travis' marriage! As he's applied this new way of life in his home, his marriage has enjoyed its own expression of transformation. In chatting about it with his lovely bride, Maddie, she has remarked how their relationship is the best it has ever been!

*****

Lars: The Marginless Media Leader

Over the last decade-and-a-half, I have had the privilege of traveling throughout the Body of Christ, both nationally and internationally. Part of the joy of those travels is meeting people who become friends and, sometimes, even teammates in advancing God's Kingdom.

On one of those trips, I met Lars, a young man who serves in media. I remember my first visit with him, enjoying his humble, hungry, and teachable heart, as well as seeing the vision he had for using his gifts and call to media for God's Kingdom. Over the next several years, Lars joined us at some of our regional d4 disciple making gatherings in Nashville, Cleveland, and Pittsburgh. I then invited him to pray about joining me in *A Leadership Journey (ALJ)*, a six-month leadership discipleship intensive that I host each year. Lars sought the Lord, got the green light, and jumped in with a dozen other men and women from around the country to participate in being shaped around God's character, ways, and mission as a leader.

One of the things we tackled together during *ALJ* was the idea of adding margin to our lives. It is something Jesus did (Mark 6:31–32), so as leaders, we need to build margin in as well. It came at a time for Lars where everything, both personally and professionally, seemed to be spilling over all the time, 100 miles per hour, all day, every day. He was exhausted, and it was impeding his productivity, mental clarity, service to God, and his overall well-being. What was particularly profound for Lars was that implementing margin into his life wasn't just for the sake of "slowing down" but really for the purpose of being available to serve God and His people, in and through his vocation.

Working in media/communications is like swimming in a constant stream of information, often with heavy waves, that never seems to stop. It's easy to be pounded by these waves of information and decisions, the processing of it all, and the demands that go with it. Implementing margin into Lars' life meant him saying "no" to some things, being more proactive with preparation, and reworking his schedule to be more generous with his time.

The fruit of applying margin in his life was immediate relief of pressure and frustration in his day-to-day activities and work. He didn't feel so rushed anymore. Lars was more available to God, not just in hearing and listening, but in serving and in having those opportunities to be available to people for whatever might be needed. It enabled him to have more peace and a clear mind to respond in his devotion, relationships, and vocational endeavors.

If you asked Lars about it today, he'd tell you that it was imperative that he become more like Jesus on this front in his life. With the wisdom of margin now applied, he would also tell you that his life is now more fruitful instead of just being full!

*****

Spence: The Enlightened Entrepreneur

Over the years, I have found that people who serve in a ministry vocation will often have a team of intercessors—those who believe their primary calling is praying for others—who regularly pray for them, their families, and their vocations. They find a regular rhythm of communication with this team, informing them of what is going on so they can cover them in prayer. I've always wondered, why doesn't every godly leader serving within every vocation have a team of intercessors who are their "go-to" pray-ers?

I was in the home of Spence, a young and creative entrepreneur who I had been discipling over the years. He showed me around his beautiful place, tucked away in the woods, and afterward, we enjoyed dinner together. As we ate, Spence shared with me about the challenges he was having with his work. Some of these issues were common to his vocation, but others seemed to me to have more "spiritual heft" to them. We had a conversation about spiritual warfare and how the enemy of our soul desires to hinder anything we do to advance God's Kingdom, better and bless the lives of others and glorify God.

Spence was familiar with the scriptural understanding of spiritual warfare. He recognized that the devil desires to "steal and kill and destroy" (John 10:10), which now included attempts to destroy what God had led him to do within his vocation.

I asked, "Do you have any intercessors who regularly pray for you and your entrepreneurial endeavors?" I could see the gears turning in his head! Spence knew that pastors, missionaries, and people in "ministry" often have intercessory prayer teams who commit to pray for them—but this was a new thought—a team praying for him in light of his role and assignment in the Kingdom of God! We talked about the value this would bring to his life and vocation, the kind of people to invite and not invite to be part of it, how to keep them current, etc. Spence saw it, caught it, and ran with it!

Spence created what he calls his Prayer Board. They've been praying for him and his business for over a decade now. It's his team who has his back as he faces business battles. He'd tell you that he has repeatedly seen miracles and divine interventions when they pray, and he considers them an absolutely vital part of his business and financial success, and Kingdom fruitfulness!

*****

Petra: The Waiting-on-the-Lord Wife

Throughout the years of our marriage, my wife, Cheryl, and I, have gone away on prayer retreats, usually at the beginning of each year and sometime during the summer months. This is a purposeful time to get away for a couple of days to seek the Lord together about our family and vocations. The aim is listening to God with the intent of obeying what He reveals to us. We take four or five two-to-three-hour segments to wait on Him about important things in our lives, challenges we are facing, and decisions we need to make. There is something truly awesome about hearing from the Lord together and walking in agreement as a couple!

When invited, we've discipled couples with a practical understanding on how to implement prayer retreats in their marriages. It has been wonderful to hear reports of what God has done as they engage this process of seeking His face as a couple.

I recently received a note from Petra, a wife of a couple who just returned from their first prayer retreat. Instead of me trying to relay it here, I think it's better that you hear directly from her!

I wanted to give you an update on our prayer retreat! WOW!!! I had no idea how much we needed this! My husband and I really believe this is something we want to do twice a year. We got much needed clarification on what God wanted to do with us in this season of our lives. We both want to say "Thank You" to you and Cheryl. Truly, your guidelines were easy to follow, and we did what God led us to do.

One of the mornings, I woke up earlier than I would for work and went out on the porch and read while God showed me his glory. IT WAS INCREDIBLE!! Also, to watch my husband be the spiritual leader of our house, take the lead and pray, read the Word, and seek God was totally awesome! I feel like if every married couple did a similar retreat for 2–3 days, to get away with no agenda, no time frame other than to check-in and check-out from where they are staying, many people would live more on the path together in Christ.

Since then, we've received answers from that prayer retreat. Answers that we both knew were from the Lord because it was exactly how He said it in scripture to us! God revealed to us areas where we needed to walk in obedience together with him. And through that came transformation!

*****

Kaleo: The Disciple Making Businessman

One day I had the opportunity to be in the office of a friend who is a leader in the food industry. Kaleo is five years my senior and was discipled by one of my spiritual sons in the Lord, who is eighteen years younger than me! I like to tease him by introducing him to a group and calling him my "grandson." People expect a little boy to run forward—only to understand when they see how much older he is than me that he is my "spiritual grandson," or third-generation disciple maker!

While visiting his office, along with seeing his company's brand, you can't help but notice "disciple making" all around you! Along with Bibles and discipleship materials on his shelves, there are various mementos representing Kaleo's own personal journey of being discipled. Looking around, you could see he was very intentional about creating a place where he could pour the ways of God into the men he was walking alongside. A nice table and some comfortable chairs offered a wonderful conversation location, and the TV was connected to show the videos accompanying *A Discipleship Journey (ADJ)*. Whether groups of guys or individual men, Kaleo had readied his workspace to do the Kingdom business of disciple making effectively! I loved it!

After being discipled, Kaleo launched his first *ADJ* group several months later with ten men. As he invested in them, he caught the bug of disciple making! He found developing special relationships with "his guys" very satisfying, having a front-row seat to see Jesus transform their lives awesome, and accelerating his spiritual development thrilling!

Over a span of six years, Kaleo has led five *ADJ* groups, taking forty guys through a year-long journey to become maturing and reproducing disciples of Jesus! He now also helps me annually facilitate the discipling of spiritual and societal leaders and serves as a great representative and reproducer of disciple making in his own church, city, and beyond!

AIMING FOR APPLICATION

1. Which story did you most identify with? Why?

2. Which story personally challenges you the most? How?

3. Do you have a vocational disciple making story that could be dropped into this chapter? If so, who is that story about and what did you disciple them in?

CHAPTER 10

Beginning with the End in Mind

Several years ago, I had the opportunity to speak at a men's regional conference hosted by Pastor Todd at his local church. He had a great turnout, with men of different backgrounds and vocations participating that weekend. I particularly remember that opening night where the Lord met the guys as they responded to a message on having "set apart hearts," committing to live their lives out of genuine humility, obedience to Jesus, serving others, and walking in the Fear of the Lord.

Prior to the conference, Pastor Todd and I had spoken several times on the phone, so this was the first occasion I was able to have some face-to-face time with him. I appreciated his pursuit of Jesus, his shepherd's heart for his precious flock, and his desire to impact his community where he lived and served. We also had some good conversation over meals, especially around things of value to both of us: family and football!

After finishing the weekend by speaking at his Sunday morning gathering, I sensed that I was to invite Pastor Todd to consider joining me in my annual six-month leadership discipleship expression, *A Leadership Journey (ALJ)*. He prayed about it and decided to jump in with about a dozen other leaders from around the country, representing various vocations and spheres of influence. *ALJ* was a time of both personal and vocational growth for him, as he learned more about God's ways and his role within His mission.

One of the pieces that he really caught and ran with was Jesus' modeling and mission of making disciple makers! Pastor Todd launched a discipleship group within his church using Lionshare's proven disciple making tool, *A Discipleship Journey (ADJ)*. Amazingly, over the next five years, he oversaw the discipling of over 300 people, which radically changed his church from the inside out! Every year now, he has a waiting list of people because of the transformation they have observed in the many lives that have been discipled.

The fruit of implementing Jesus' style of disciple making has also resulted in a congregational DNA conversion. As a flock, they have doubled in size, adding new leaders, some even going on to receive their ministry credentials. Both their monthly and missions giving have tripled, allowing them to make an even greater impact both locally and globally, including partnering in planting nineteen new churches around the world!

Through his vocational calling, Pastor Todd has committed to obeying Jesus' command to make disciples. It took him four years of faithfully staying the course, working hard, and investing deeply, but the spiritual fruit has been transformative, both for him and for the flock he dearly loves. Now, he takes joy in watching those he's discipled effectively reproduce the life of Jesus in others! And I take great joy in watching his flock actively advance God's Kingdom truly better and bless the lives of others and wonderfully glorify God!

*****

We've considered much about calling and vocation and their link to the Great Co-Mission and disciple making in our lives. It's now up to you to apply these core Kingdom realities into your life, relationships, and vocation. However, before we bring this book to an end, there is something of great importance I need to share with you.

When I was twenty-three years old, something was deposited in me by a godly leader that became a core part of my thinking and remains so to this day: *beginning with the end in mind.* This taught me to always reference the "end game" from the Scriptures and what Jesus had put in my heart to do. It has kept me focused on what's most important, motivated me to view everything through the eyes of eternity, and has oriented me through the great ups and downs of life.

So, while getting on with connecting our calling and the Great Co-Mission, what is the scriptural "end game" that we must consistently reference as we go about our Father's business? Here are three that I would submit we must set our eyes upon, day-in-and-day-out.

Advancing God's Kingdom

A read-through of the Gospels reveals that the core message of Jesus is the Kingdom of God. In the Sermon on the Mount, in Matthew 5–7, Jesus shares much about His Kingdom. In looking at this portion over the years, two truths from Matthew 6 have always served me well as a reference point regarding the Kingdom.

The first one appears in Jesus' teaching on prayer in verse 10: *Your kingdom come, your will be done, on Earth as it is in heaven.* So, what's going on in heaven that God desires to have expressed here on Earth?

Most significantly, God's character and ways are on full display! Heaven is the dwelling place of the *Lord God Almighty, who was, and is, and is to come!* The angels and all the residents of heaven—including those who've arrived ahead of us—see Him for Who He really is! The main attraction of heaven is the King Himself! Jesus intends that His character and ways be reflected through us on Earth just as He is revealed in heaven.

Heaven is also the home of God's will always being done. As "Carriers of His Kingdom" here in this world, we need to be seeking God with all our hearts to know what He desires to do within our situations at home, in our communities, and within our vocations. As in heaven, so on Earth!

The second truth is found in verse 33, where Jesus said, *Seek first the Kingdom of God and His righteousness, and all these things will be added to you.* During His life, Jesus did everything with His eyes on the Kingdom: living it, teaching it, demonstrating it, building it, advancing it, and multiplying it.

Seeking first the Kingdom of God means we are paying attention to what He is up to in the various settings and relationships that He has placed us in, and then cooperating with what it is that He wants to do. As Dr. Henry Blackaby says in his book *Experiencing*

God, "Watch to see where God is working and join Him."[1] When we see what God is doing, we can join Him with our time, gifts, and resources to advance His Kingdom, while at the same time, cheering on others who are serving the Kingdom on different fronts, in different ways!

Speaking of different fronts and ways, a kingdom perspective also doesn't allow insecurities and comparisons to cloud what God is doing. Let me illustrate what I mean by this.

Let's say God is doing great work in your city through a young adult group from another church that is meeting a real need among the poor. A Kingdom perspective means you don't compare, devalue it with your words, or become insecure and threatened because it wasn't your church's idea. Instead, you seek how you can serve it. When you have a Kingdom perspective it doesn't matter what person/company/group/church puts "points on the Kingdom scoreboard," because as "Kingdom players" we're all on the same team!

So, when you are getting ready for the day, are you also preparing to reference how you might be able to advance God's Kingdom in your family, friendships, in your community, and in and through your vocation?

Bettering and Blessing the Lives of People

Look with me at this passage in Acts 10:38; it tells us,

> *...how God anointed Jesus of Nazareth with the Holy Spirit and with power. He went about doing good and healing all who were oppressed by the devil, for God was with him.*

We are familiar with the truth that Jesus was anointed with the Holy Spirit and power to heal the blind, lame, sick, oppressed, etc.

But did you know, in the context of this verse, that He was just as anointed with the Holy Spirit and power to do good?

Doing good!

Sometimes I think we forget (or maybe never learned?) the truth that God is good and that the natural inclination of His Father's heart is always to bless people. Goodness is part of God's character; it's who He is!

Jesus carried within Him the sincere desire to better and bless the lives of people He met. Bettering their lives by meeting real needs and blessing their lives by extending grace (getting what one hasn't earned nor deserves) and favor (benefits given based on God's good pleasure).

When Jesus was in the synagogue on a Sabbath in Nazareth, he took the scroll of Isaiah, stood up and read this, declaring that it was being fulfilled through Him on that very day.

The Spirit of the Lord is upon me, because he has anointed me to proclaim good news to the poor. He has sent me to proclaim liberty to the captives and recovering of sight to the blind, to set at liberty those who are oppressed, to proclaim the year of the Lord's favor. (Luke 4:18–19)

Here, again, we see the Holy Spirit's empowering behind Jesus' "doing good"!

- Proclaiming good news to the poor
- Proclaiming liberty to the captives
- Recovering of sight to the blind
- Setting at liberty those who are oppressed
- Proclaiming the year of the Lord's favor

Picture what that must have been like for each one who was on the receiving end of these expressions of bettering and blessing! Imagine the emotions of freedom, relief, joy, gladness, hope, and sheer amazement that must have encompassed their hearts! But it doesn't stop there. Consider the impact on their families and friends who had loved, served, and were perhaps required for years to take care of them.

Poverty, captivity, physical suffering, and spiritual oppression lifted away! All gone.

The Gospels contain a ton of examples where we see the goodness of Jesus on behalf of others. I want to focus here on some expressions that may not seem quite as "spiritual" as the ones listed in Luke 4, but nonetheless were just as "good" to those on the receiving end!

- When 5,000 and 4,000 people (likely the count of men, not including women and children) were hungry and away from their homes, Jesus made sure they all ate (Matthew 14:13–21, 15:32–28)!

- At a wedding, when either the servants were panicking or the happy couple was on the verge of embarrassment because of no more wine to drink, Jesus quietly provided for them and their guests (John 2:1–11)!

- Peter, Thomas, Nathanael, James, John, and two other disciples who had failed to catch anything after being out fishing all night—at the direction of Jesus to cast the net on the right side of the boat—literally caught a boatload of large fish, 153 to be exact! A very personalized expression of goodness by Jesus to the heart of Peter, who was likely still recovering from his denial a few weeks before (John 21:4–8).

- While passing through Jericho, Jesus saw the town's "short tax man," Zacchaeus, up high in a tree. He called him by name and invited Himself over to his house for lunch. Although probably highly criticized by the people in town, Jesus bettered and blessed Zacchaeus' life by publicly identifying with him and going into his home, not to mention what happened once they got in there (Luke 19:1–10)!

- In the Garden of Gethsemane, shortly after recording that Jesus was sweating great drops of blood, Judas and the crowd arrive to arrest Him. During the arrest, Peter (John 18:10) cuts off the right ear of the servant of the high priest. Jesus touches his ear and heals him. Got to think that gesture of bettering his life was transformative for him (Luke 22:47–51)!

- And then there's the story of the Good Samaritan. A man is stripped and beaten by robbers, leaving him half dead. Several spiritually influential folks—a priest and Levite— pass on by and do nothing. But a Samaritan—the last person those listening to the story would think of doing this—had compassion, bound up his wounds, took him to an inn, and paid for his care! The little "doing goods" that many don't want to do, and others won't likely see, are a huge expression, according to Jesus, of bettering and blessing other's lives (Luke 10:25–37).

Where has God provided you with a vocational advantage to steward as an opportunity to change another's disadvantage? Where are there systemic issues – racial, economic, lack of opportunity – that you can bring into greater scriptural alignment with justice and equity?

When you are going about your day, are you aware of and make margin for the moments that Jesus sets up for you to better and bless the lives of others?

Glorifying God

When I was twelve and thirteen years of age, I participated in my church's catechism classes, led by our pastor. As part of our learning, the question was asked, "What is the chief end of man?" The answer to that question was,

"To glorify God and enjoy Him forever."

Did you know that the single focused aim of Jesus is to bring glory to His Heavenly Father? Glorifying God is the heartbeat of the Kingdom. During His prayer in John 17:4, Jesus said,

I glorified you on earth, having accomplished the work that you gave me to do.

Jesus carried within Him a deep concern about the reputation for the name that He represented regarding the work that God had given Him to do.

To catch the weight of what it means to glorify God, a little background here might help.

In Jesus' time, people's reputations and the authority they carried were directly connected to their names. Their characters, actions, words, people skills, business dealings, and other attributes either significantly enhanced or severely damaged their reputations in the eyes of others. A person's name and reputation were inseparable.

The Scriptures teach us that how His name is handled is of enormous importance to God.

The fourth of the Ten Commandments says, *You shall not take the name of the Lord your God in vain, for the Lord will not hold him guiltless who takes his name in vain* (Exodus 20:7). Somehow this command is often reduced to only mean we should not use God's name as a swear word. There is eternally more meaning to it than that. In Hebrew, vain is the word *shav*, meaning "emptiness, vanity, falsehood." When we live in a way that distorts—make empty or false—who God really is and what He's really like, it results in giving God's name a bad reputation!

Leviticus 19:12 reads, *You shall not swear by my name falsely, and so profane the name of your God...* In Hebrew, the word for profane is *chalaland*, which means "to defile, pollute, desecrate, to make common, to violate the honor of." The people of God need to be careful not to profane, pollute or dishonor God's name and reputation, not only because it maligns and misrepresents Him, but also because it hinders His name from being spread throughout the earth!

Jesus understood the ramifications of keeping God's name and reputation always "on His radar." He realized that misappropriating God's name would be catastrophic. When people of different ethnicities or faiths have been killed over the centuries "in the name of Jesus," God's reputation is wounded and His name profaned. When followers of Jesus say one thing but live the exact opposite, it wounds the reputation of God, hindering the momentum of the Kingdom. When trusted godly leaders betray the name they carry through how they live and lead, the fallout often results in irreparable damage. I've watched it firsthand.

Weighty stuff, huh?

So, how can we elevate God's name and reputation through our lives in our world today?

First, I like Leith Anderson's practical way of expressing it: "Living to the glory of God means living in such a way that we enhance the reputation of God in the eyes of others."[2] Imagine if we approached our words, decisions, relationships, and vocations through the grid of, "Am I enhancing God's reputation in the eyes of others?" We glorify God when we live our lives so that people see and are drawn to the beauty and wonder of who He really is. They see His character in our lives. They are won to His ways through our lives. And, they want to find their mission, as they watch you fulfill yours!

So, whether you eat or drink, or whatever you do, do all to the glory of God. (1 Corinthians 10:31)

And, second, we need to go back to the other half of the answer to the chief end of man: *enjoy Him forever*. I have discovered that part of glorifying God in our lives is enjoying Him through our lives! Most followers of Jesus I know sincerely love, worship, and serve Him. However, it is rare that I run across those who have learned how to enjoy Him.

I really like John Piper's wonderful insight and comment on this: "God is most glorified in us when we are most satisfied in Him."[3]

Check out these verses with me,

Delight yourself in the Lord, and He will give you the desires of your heart. (Psalm 37:4)

Then I will go to the altar of God, to God my exceeding joy... (Psalm 43:4)

...for the joy of the Lord is your strength. (Nehemiah 8:10)

In the first Psalm of David, the word *delight* means to "take exquisite delight," while the word *joy* in the second is the Hebrew word for "gladness, glee, and pleasure." The word *joy* in Nehemiah is a third Hebrew word speaking of "gladness and joy."

As we enjoy God by taking exquisite delight, gladness, and pleasure in His character, ways, and works, our hearts become further intertwined with His. And, while He gives us the desires of heart, our own hearts are filled with a longing to fulfill His!

I've found a number of ways in Scripture, and by practice, to more fully enjoy God. I'd like to share several with you here.

First, just as I enjoy my friends more by experiencing more of their character, I've found the same to be true in my relationship with God. Read the Scriptures with an eye for His names, titles, and attributes. Reflect on them. Dig in a little deeper by searching for that attribute throughout the Scriptures. Watch as God will reveal more of this aspect through your daily life. Tie it into your worship, and strongly declare the truth of who He is in light of your life circumstances. Try it, and you'll find yourself enjoying Him even more!

Another way I enjoy God is by pausing to be more intentional to appreciate His creation around me. Just as soon-to-be-parents fuss over the nursery in their home for their new baby, so God has "fussed over His creation" for our pleasure! Everything from pounding waves to wild thunderstorms, the beauty of sunsets, and the countless stars in the night sky (of which He knows each by name!). The many kinds of animals, birds of the air, and amazing sea life beneath the ocean. Cheryl and I always enjoy the beauty and bounty of Minnesota's many lakes and rivers. Take it all in; He made it just for you! See His hand behind it all and enjoy!

I've got to share one more.

With our lives being so busy, we often miss enjoying God's intervening and transforming the lives of others or working on behalf of others. As I pay more attention to God setting hearts free, maturing us in His ways, bringing people across our paths, opening doors that were once shut, and providing undeserved blessings, I can't help but connect the dots! And, when I do, they all point straight back to Him! Sometimes my heart or smiling mouth will say, "I see you and what you're doing…"! Watch, connect the dots, and enjoy!

As you begin your day, do you reference how you might "enhance the reputation of God in the eyes of others"? When was the last time or how will you begin to more intentionally enjoy God?

Bookends

It's appropriate that we wind up here. Like bookends, we began looking at connecting, calling, and co-missioning through the life of Isaiah's seeing God, and now we close with enjoying Him. Our seeing and enjoying God—our friendship and walk with God—needs always to hold the center place of our hearts. It needs to be actively cultivated, tended, refreshed, and, at times, revived. It's only out of the overflow of our friendship with God that we are able to do what He's called us to do.

Without it, nothing else matters, works, or even fits. As eternally important as our vocational callings and Great Co-Mission disciple making endeavors are, without Jesus being our first love, even those things can subtly become idols of our hearts, thus moving us sideways instead of in God's ways.

Thanks for taking this journey with me.

Now...

Here's to you seeing and enjoying Jesus more than ever.

And, embracing the shaping of God in your life and His sending you into your appointed vocational calling while making disciple makers that will reproduce God's character, ways, and mission for generations to come.

So that in the end, God's Kingdom will be advanced, people's lives will be bettered and blessed, and the name of Jesus will be name glorified.

This is the great opportunity!

About the Author

D ave Buehring is a devoted disciple of Jesus who is engaged in equipping the Church, guiding leaders, and reproducing disciple makers.

Over four-plus decades, Dave has led on local, national, and international fronts. He has had the opportunity to speak thousands of times in hundreds of settings, including conferences and retreats, leadership summits, vocational venues, churches, schools and universities, and humanitarian aid trainings.

He is often found walking alongside leaders of all ages, who lead throughout the vocations. Referencing wisdom from the Scriptures, blended with his broad experiences, he guides them toward living godly lives and leading in the ways of God.

Dave is the Founder and President of Lionshare (www. Lionshare.org), a nonprofit organization aimed at igniting and equipping churches and vocational leaders to fulfill Jesus' Great Co-Mission of making disciple makers. He's the author of *A Discipleship Journey*, a scripturally sound, proven, and practical disciple making resource used throughout the United States and in numerous nations throughout the world since 2004. Dave annually hosts A Leadership Journey, a six-month leadership intensive for spiritual and societal leaders. He also can be regularly heard on Lionshare's podcast *Wisdom Unlocked: The Ways of God*.

He has the privilege of participating on the pastoral team at his home church, Grace Chapel, and has been a part of an international community of leaders, Messenger Fellowship, for over thirty years.

Dave and his wife, Cheryl, reside in the beautiful hills of Franklin, Tennessee, where they enjoy spending time with their family and friends.

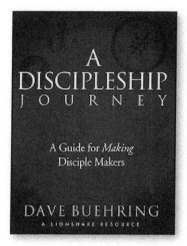

A DISCIPLESHIP JOURNEY
A Guide for Making Disciple Makers

A Discipleship Journey (ADJ) is a deliberate ONE YEAR pathway of transformation towards living more like Jesus and joining His disciple making mission. You will learn about knowing God's character, hearing His voice, becoming a godly and healthy relater and finding your role on God's team. Materials include an ADJ manual, online weekly videos and a facilitator's guide for small group application.
Coming soon: ADJ Kids Edition!

VOCATIONAL DISCIPLE MAKING GUIDES
A Tool to Transform Your Work World

A follow-up to *The Great Opportunity,* Lionshare's Vocational Disciple Making Guides are created to help you make disciples of those who work in your field. Over ten weeks, you'll catch God's perspective on your vocation and how you can fulfill His purposes in and through it each day.

VOCATIONAL
DISCIPLE MAKING GUIDES

A Tool to *Transform*
Your Work World

LIONSHARE
A LIONSHARE RESOURCE

WELCOME TO THE KINGDOM
A Thirty Day Journey to Ground New Believers in Their Faith

Welcome to the Kingdom is geared towards grounding new followers of Jesus in the values of God's Kingdom, connecting them to the scriptures and His Church, while introducing them to God's character and sharing Him with their family and friends. It's a great tool for further-along followers to help new believers take their first steps of faith.

A LEADERSHIP JOURNEY
Shaping Leaders in the Ways of God

Our changing times require a different kind of leader. Led by Dave Buehring, *A Leadership Journey* is a SIX MONTH experience for leaders who desire to live and lead more like Jesus within their vocations. Themes include building healthy margins in your life and relationships, becoming the kind of leader that others want to follow, gaining seasoned wisdom from the scriptures, discovering God's story in and through your life and finding a compass for finishing well.

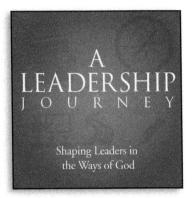

To learn more about Lionshare and our other resources, including the *Wisdom Unlocked* podcast, free eBooks, daily devotionals, video teachings, and hosting d4 conferences visit **www.Lionshare.org**.

Endnotes

Introduction
1. Barna Group, *Christians at Work: Examining the Intersection of Calling & Career* (2018), 18.
2. Barna Group, *Christians at Work: Examining the Intersection of Calling & Career* (2018), 49.
3. Barna Group, *Christians at Work: Examining the Intersection of Calling & Career* (2018), 25.

Chapter 1
1. Barna Group, *Christians at Work: Examining the Intersection of Calling & Career* (2018), 19.
2. Barna Group, *Christians at Work: Examining the Intersection of Calling & Career* (2018), 30.
3. Barna Group, *Christians at Work: Examining the Intersection of Calling & Career* (2018), 17.
4. Ibid.

Chapter 2

1. Bobby Clinton. Accessed February 20, 2020. http://bobbyclinton.com/store/articles/.

Chapter 3

1. O. E. Feucht, *Everyone a Minister* (St. Louis: Concordia, 1979), 80.
2. Jack Hayford, *Conversations with Fathers of the Faith*. DVD. Franklin: Lionshare Leadership Group, 2009.
3. Martin Luther, Henry Eyster Jacobs, Adolph Spaeth, *Works of Martin Luther* (A.J. Holman Company, 1915).
4. Gene Edward Veith (1999), "The Doctrine of Vocation: How God Hides Himself in Human Work," *Modern Reformation*, May/June 1999, Vol: 8, Num: 3.
5. Ibid.
6. Ibid.
7. Ibid.
8. "Facts on Noah's Ark and the Flood." Christian Information Ministries. Accessed February 20, 2020. http://www.ldolphin.org/cisflood.html.

Chapter 4

1. David Padfield, "God and Government," 2005. PDF File. https://www.padfield.com/acrobat/sermons/civil_government.pdf
2. Ibid.
3. O. Pedersen, "Galileo's Religion." The SAO/NASA Astrophysics Data System, 1985. http://adsabs.harvard.edu/full/1985gamf.conf...75P, 90.
4. Dave Armstrong, *Science and Christianity: Close Partners or Mortal Enemies?* (Dave Armstrong, 2012).
5. Ibid.
6. "Man on the Moon: Technology Then and Now." IT Pro. July 9, 2009. Accessed February 20, 2020. https://www.itpro.co.uk/612913/man-on-the-moon-technology-then-and-now.

Chapter 5

1. Dr. Glenn R. Martin, *Biblical Christian Education: Liberation for Leadership*. PDF File. https://www.biblicalchristianworld-view.net/documents/biblicalChristianLeadershipGlennMartin.pdf, 7.
2. Robert J. Banks, R. Paul Stevens, *The Marketplace Ministry Handbook: A Manual for Work, Money and Business* (Regent College Publishing, 2005).
3. Hans Schwarz, *True Faith in the True God: An Introduction to Luther's Life and Thought* (Minneapolis: Augsburg Books, 1996), 24.

Chapter 6

1. Barna Group, *Christians at Work: Examining the Intersection of Calling & Career* (2018), 60–61.

Chapter 8

1. "World Population Projected to Reach 9.8 Billion in 2050, and 11.2 Billion in 2100 | UN DESA Department of Economic and Social Affairs." United Nations. United Nations, June 21, 2017. Accessed February 20, 2020. https://www.un.org/development/desa/en/news/population/world-population-prospects-2017.html.
2. Grant Edwards, July 13, 2019. Accessed February 20, 2020. http://www.grantedwardsauthor.com.

Chapter 10

1. Henry Blackaby, *Experiencing God: Knowing and Doing the Will of God* (Nashville: LifeWay Press, 1993).
2. Leith Anderson, *A Church for the 21st Century* (Minneapolis: Bethany House Publishers, 1992).
3. John Piper. "God Is Most Glorified in Us When We Are Most Satisfied in Him." *Desiring God* (blog), October 13, 2012. Accessed February 20, 2020. https://www.desiringgod.org/

messages/god-is-most-glorified-in-us-when-we-are-most-satisfied-in-him.

CPSIA information can be obtained
at www.ICGtesting.com
Printed in the USA
JSHW021024090321
12388JS00003B/126

9 781631 951794